Character in the
American Experience

POLITICAL THEORY FOR TODAY

Series Editor: Richard Avramenko, University of Wisconsin, Madison

Political Theory for Today seeks to bring the history of political thought out of the jargon-filled world of the academy into the everyday world of social and political life. The series brings the wisdom of texts and the tradition of political philosophy to bear on salient issues of our time, especially issues pertaining to human freedom and responsibility, the relationship between individuals and the state, the moral implications of public policy, health and human flourishing, public and private virtues, and more. Great thinkers of the past have thought deeply about the human condition and their situations—books in Political Theory for Today build on that insight.

Titles Published

Idolizing the Idea: A Critical History of Modern Philosophy by
  Wayne Cristaudo
Eric Voegelin Today: Voegelin's Political Thought in the 21st Century,
  edited by Scott Robinson, Lee Trepanier, David Whitney

Character in the American Experience

An Unruly People

Bruce P. Frohnen and Ted V. McAllister

LEXINGTON BOOKS
Lanham • Boulder • New York • London

Published by Lexington Books
An imprint of The Rowman & Littlefield Publishing Group, Inc.
4501 Forbes Boulevard, Suite 200, Lanham, Maryland 20706
www.rowman.com

86-90 Paul Street, London EC2A 4NE

British Library Cataloguing in Publication Information Available

Library of Congress Cataloging-in-Publication Data

Names: Frohnen, Bruce, author. | McAllister, Ted V., author.
Title: Character in the American experience: an unruly people / Bruce P. Frohnen and
    Ted V. McAllister.
Other titles: Unruly people
Description: Lanham: Lexington Books, [2022] | Series: Political theory for today |
    Includes bibliographical references and index.
Identifiers: LCCN 2022037257 (print) | LCCN 2022037258 (ebook)
    | ISBN 9781666914504 (cloth) | ISBN 9781666914528 (paper) | ISBN
    9781666914511 (ebook)
Subjects: LCSH: National characteristics, American—History. | Political culture—United
    States—History.
Classification: LCC E169.1 .F863 2022 (print) | LCC E169.1 (ebook) | DDC 973—dc23/
    eng/20220815
LC record available at https://lccn.loc.gov/2022037257
LC ebook record available at https://lccn.loc.gov/2022037258

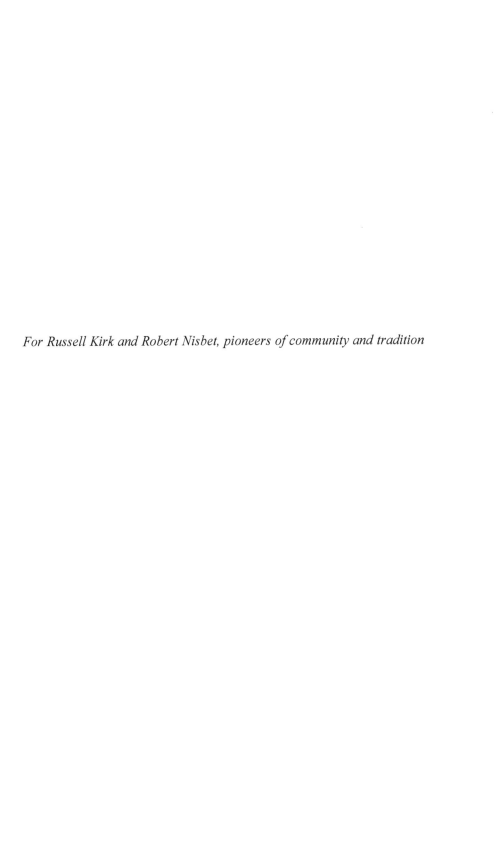

For Russell Kirk and Robert Nisbet, pioneers of community and tradition

Contents

Introduction

SELF, CHARACTER, AND PEOPLE

What makes us American? Neither blood nor ideology but human relationships have made us who we are. To fully understand ourselves we must look at how we relate to one another—how we come together, how we argue, and why. For centuries, Americans have banded together to found towns, set up businesses, worship God, and address the most practical local issues. Also for centuries, Americans have made their often overlapping and even competing communities work together, forming a common way of life that maintained the integrity of its component parts and emphasized the virtues of self-government. The sources of this strange genius are many and diverse, but can be summed up in our national motto, *e pluribus unum*—out of many, one.

Unfortunately, our understanding of *e pluribus unum* has been muddied over time, leading people to think that forming a single United States somehow meant rejecting the primary communities in which Americans have always lived, developed their most important relationships, and learned the art of association. In America, the one was not designed to replace, but rather to include the many. Indeed, the one—meaning the nation as a whole—by nature seeks to protect the many, the natural communities in which healthy peoples form and thrive.

What is more, America has always been a land of disagreement and conflict between individuals, families, and communities; we have been an unruly people. Americans have been different from other peoples because we refused to prioritize any one association above all the others. Families are important, but most Americans have rejected clan politics and the kinds of family-based corruption all too common throughout the world. We have treated religion much the same way, holding our faiths dear but cooperating or competing with members of other faiths depending on the object of concern or danger we face. And most of us have been proud to call ourselves American, but often at least as proud to say we are Ohioans, Oklahomans, or Californians,

1

or that our ancestors were from England, or Germany, or Mexico, or Nigeria (or all four). Our communities, like our loyalties, overlap and sometimes pull in different directions. But it has been the tension we experience in multiple communities—the combination of cooperation, competition, and low-level conflict—that has kept those communities vibrant and kept us both grounded and free.

This book brings together stories of American people and communities. Stories of founding, conflict, and cooperation. Our goal is to give readers a chance to consider how Americans once managed to cooperate, compete, and sometimes fight, in ways that shaped who we are, in ourselves, in our communities, and as a people. The book is organized as a history of the American character. It focuses on essential moments in our development as a people, from the Puritan landing in the New World to the American Revolution and development of a new, constitutional government, through the Civil War, the failure of Reconstruction, to the rise of a distinctly American form of Progressivism that brought the formation of a mass administrative state, through the radicalism of the Vietnam era to current conflicts over globalization and the demand for a social democratic government focused on grievances rooted in race, sex, and sexual orientation. But our emphasis is less on the grand sweep of history than on the actions and reactions of American communities. Thus, we look at the forging of the original colonies, the problems for all Americans posed by slavery, the religious revivals that forged American character, and the changes in that character wrought by military and social conflict. As important, though, are the stories of settlement, of the formation of communities by America's exceptional men and women, and the seemingly spontaneous order that spawned movements, countermovements, and entire cities, like Oklahoma City, seemingly from scratch.

The continuities in forms of life and interaction are as important as the changes in overall character. The ability of state and federal administrators to "lock down" America in response to fears of pandemic may signal a fundamental change in American character, a new acceptance of elite opinion and administrative power. The steady increase in reliance on government programs to keep us safe from poverty, disease, and the consequences of various foolish actions (whether our own or those of others) may have made us less unruly and more compliant. Still, much of America continues to demand self-rule and show some willingness to fight for it, even as the dark side of our unruliness—an openness to criminal activity—seems resurgent. Conflict continues so long as America continues.

One hears much about how America is coming apart and, sadly, there appears to be much truth to it. But it is important to remember that Americans have always been prone to a certain amount of unrest, of more general restlessness, and to resisting the call to "unity" out of a determination to maintain their own self-government. For many of us, too strident a call for unity demands that we give up our deep identity as Americans in exchange for a safety that exists more in theory than in fact given the limits on our ability to make the world, and its people, conform to our plans and desires.

To the extent Americans have been bound together it has been less in unison than in conversation. Interlocking and overlapping relationships and loyalties have existed within a culture shaped by competing religious visions and a sense of our own character dominated by differing dispositions. American culture is the product of competing biblical religions, differing in doctrine and religious practice, but agreeing on more fundamental norms and especially the reality of human dignity and sin. American character was forged by a dynamic tension between the independent individualist and the responsible citizen—between the reckless adventurer and the duty-bound yeoman, the outlaw and the lawman. George Washington, father of our country, was also a rebel against the British Empire. Wyatt Earp was arrested several times in his youth, including for horse stealing, yet grew to become one of our best-known lawmen. Both earned praise by putting their lives on the line for the public good. The creative tension between independence and duty, as between different religions and traditions, fostered action in the public square in pursuit of truth, honor, public respect, and the common good.

Then there are American politics. For over a century now, analysts and activists have told us that our politics are divided between the forces of progress and reaction. This unbalanced view, usually imparted by Progressive partisans, is sometimes put forward by pessimistic scholars on the right. Clinton Rossiter in the 1950s termed Conservatism "the thankless persuasion" on account of its (to him natural and essential) role as a partial brake on the dynamism of those marching America forward. But "forward" toward what? Toward ever greater individual autonomy and group security, toward a society enforcing what one might term "libertarian socialism," in which individuals choose whatever "lifestyle" they desire, secure in the belief that government institutions will save them from physical, financial, and even psychological danger. In more recent years critical race theorists, Black Lives Matter activists, and antifa rioters all have demanded that we destroy the way of life we inherited so that we can "progress" toward a race-based society administered by an all-inclusive set of institutions parceling out money, jobs, and respect.

How did we get to the point where so many in positions of power and authority are calling for our society and people to be replaced? We lost track of the fact that politics are not what make us American. We forgot that our politics flow from our culture and our sense of who we are as persons and people. We hid from ourselves how powerfully our own characters, and the characters of our communities, shape how and how well we live.

For two generation we have been taught, not to revere, but to resent or forcibly co-opt our elders. Over the last several decades, histories of early America have tended to fall into one of two camps. One condemns our predecessors as hateful despots who built the oppressive institutions from which only contemporary academics and activists can free us. The other seeks to "vindicate" our forebears as good progressives-in-the-making who did their best to set up modern, individualist institutions and succeeded in laying the groundwork for political and cultural modernization. Neither group seeks to understand Americans as they were, let alone as they understood themselves. In this brief volume we can't hope to correct all such errors so long in the making. But we can work to see behind contemporary prejudices to our forebears' way of life. That way of life, and the self-understanding that went with it, was rooted in neither hunger for power nor selfish individualism. It shared with all human institutions and societies an unfortunate amount of abuse, and of unjust animosity and self-serving denigration of various groups. But it remained rooted in a coherent vision of the common good and the virtues necessary for a decent society of self-governing people.

A central cause of our current discontents is the loss, or rejection, by many people in America of what it means to be fully human. What is a person? Is it a matter of race, of sex, of mere choice or will? If choice is the key, then who or what is doing the choosing? Such questions, recently brought to a crisis point, are in fact quite old, and have been crucial to American public life for many decades. In the past we addressed them with courage and conviction. It is time to look at them anew, reaching for those same virtues that served us in the past.

THE ENDANGERED SELF

"What is the American Character?" asked *Time* magazine on its cover in September of 1954. The issue featured scholar David Riesman, whose 1950 book *The Lonely Crowd*[1] was arguably the most important and influential work of social science in the decades following World War II. The question of "American character" seemed urgent in those years, as though Americans were confronting an existential threat as a nation, a society, and a culture. Underneath it all was a more foundational question: Had America already lost its character or been transformed?

The anxiety attending these questions sprang from many sources and went in myriad directions. The experiences of the war, and particularly of Nazi concentration camps, provoked a variety of moral and sociological conundrums, all associated with a larger historical trend that went under the label "modernity." The heart of the issue, of course, was the inescapable fact (pressed on Americans by the unprecedented nature of so much of recent history) that the present and the future looked radically different from the not-so-distant past. It all felt like a rupture, a discontinuity that suddenly seemed an inevitable trajectory: a strong current sweeping them toward some strange destiny that they now strained to see more clearly.

Were the concentration camps, and the hideous ideological systems that made them and the Soviet gulags possible, more than just the most recent historical outrage? Did they represent something new, embedded in the emerging reality of modernity, that showed in grotesque form the kinds of emerging systems already swallowing up the peoples of the world, even Americans?

Much mid-century anxiety focused on the status of the individual person under modern conditions. The dehumanizing effects on people subjected to the brutal, totalitarian control of the concentration camp raised questions about whether a softer form of dehumanization was taking place in our social system. The scholarly analyses that proceeded along these lines explored everything from the psychological effects of slavery to Betty Friedan's famous claim that the American housewife lived in a "comfortable concentration camp." An outpouring of scholarly and cultural works supplied ample and remarkably similar expressions of a shared anxiety about social control over the individual self.

Deep concern over increasing conformism combined with a newly urgent obsession with roots as old as Tocqueville's *Democracy in America*: the tendency toward infantilizing American adults. The result was serious doubt about whether there remained a sustainable American character. Riesman supplied the most convincing analysis, at least among intellectuals of the 1950s. More, he created a typology that would help make sense of the changing nature and implications of the American character. Americans of the nineteenth century had been "inner-directed," but by 1950 a new personality type had become dominant—the "other-directed" person. Prior to both types, historically, was the "tradition-directed" person who, for Riesman, essentially fell outside the American experience.

The inner-directed person was a producer, a creator, a mover and shaker. He (and it was largely men about whom Riesman wrote) was the archetype of the self-reliant person who had deeply internalized his moral beliefs from his parents and the primary institutions of his youth. Knowing right from wrong, with this knowledge a constitutive part of his being, the inner-directed man did not depend on social cues to determine his actions. Riesman suggested that he operated with a moral "gyroscope" that helped him measure, understand, and assess his environment and to act consistent with his internal moral constitution.

Similar in many respects to Max Weber's man of the Protestant Ethic, the inner-directed man took full responsibility for his actions and fate, seeing his environment as filled with opportunities for the person who worked hard, took hardship as part of life, and believed that work rather than play was the core of real identity. As historian Wilfred McClay puts it, "Inner direction was appropriate to the era of capitalist expansion. In a production-oriented age ruled by the psychology of scarcity, the force of productive labor was concentrated on conquering 'the hardness of material,' work and play were severely differentiated, and pleasure was a 'sideshow,' a fleeting escape from care that principally served to refresh the individual for a return to life's battle."[2]

Such a personality type produces explorers, settlers, builders, and all the "types" that we associate (or used to associate) with the best expressions of "the American character." But it seemed that modernity had made the inner-directed man obsolete. In his place Riesman described the rise of the other-directed person who lacked a gyroscope but possessed a kind of social radar. Radar sends out signals that bounce back to form a picture of the world outside oneself. The other-directed person was, therefore, characterized by his ability to read the social environment and conform to it or, for the most successful among them, conform to society's emerging trends and beliefs. No longer equipped with an internalized and stable moral constitution, the other-directed person adapted himself to the moral beliefs of society or, at least, his peer group. To be successful an other-directed person had to be very sensitive and responsive to changes in social norms. As a parent or a teacher in a society of other-directed persons one must prepare the child for success by helping him to adjust to evolving moral norms and social behavior. A fixed moral constitution was the enemy of social success. In an age of mass entertainment and therefore mass advertising, the other-directed person learned a deep consumerism—not simply a desire to buy more but a belief that one's identity and sense of self were tied to what one consumed, to corporate brands that supplied visible, social expressions of taste, choice, and thereby identity. The other-directed person was less an entrepreneur and more a "company man," less a producer and more a consumer, less an explorer and more a tourist.

In the context of the Cold War, as the United States struggled against a totalitarian system of control, the other-directed person represented a failure of the American system, a weakness in the struggle. A consumer-based moral relativism provides no way to defeat an ideologically driven enemy. On this, at least, the right and the left seemed to agree. What was to be done?

Just three months after *Time* asked "What is the American Character," a huge chunk of America affirmed an answer offered by Walt Disney. On December 15, 1954, CBS aired *Davy Crockett, Indian Fighter*, a mythologizing of the quintessential inner-directed man, presented fully equipped with the set of virtues that made America great. The reception of this TV movie and its two sequels was not only unexpected by those who made these children's dramas but utterly unprecedented in American popular culture. Indeed, Crockett had largely been forgotten by the 1950s, except in Texas, where his death at the Alamo earned him a place in their memory. Disney himself was very reluctant to produce a miniseries on Crockett, but a bit of research revealed a rich if largely forgotten stash of stories and tall tales about this frontiersman, Congressman, and hero of the Alamo—many published by Davy himself in his autobiography and elsewhere. In retrospect, Crockett's life and legend served brilliantly as raw material for a television hero. Whatever the hard facts, the stories Davy and his admirers told were all straight out of the American book of virtues, writ large and made colorful.

The motto of Davy's autobiography, "Be sure that you're right, then go ahead," represented the defining idea of a self-reliant and self-governing person and became the constant refrain in the TV series. Here was a man who could never be influenced by the majority, by social pressure, nor by some authority or power that told him to do something that violated his moral constitution, his governing principles. Brave, sincere, and loyal, perhaps no trait was more important to the Crockett character than his honesty, for honesty was the cornerstone virtue of an American species of honor. In one example of this expression of honor, Davy was involved in the war with the Creek Indians—in this case a rump group of Creeks led by Red Stick. While part of the American military effort in this war (for Davy always showed his willingness to fight and die for the cause of freedom), Crockett only followed orders when they squared with his motto, ignoring those he considered illegitimate.

The themes of honor and character were highlighted in a fight (man-to-man) between him and Red Stick. Throughout this episode Davy had expressed sympathy for the American Indian (something that would be highlighted in the next episode, where he fought President Jackson over the removal of the Cherokee Indians from their land—"Injuns got rights, they're folks like everyone else") and had balanced his admiration for the Indian way of life with the universal appeal of the rule of law as understood in the US Constitution. But in response to a massacre led by Red Stick, Davy had joined the cause and now, months later, the two men were fighting hand to hand. Crockett got the best of Red Stick but stopped short of killing him and instead appealed to Red Stick's reason to save his people from further deaths. Red Stick, frustrated by the US government's tendency to violate treaties, said "White government lies." Crockett did not deny this and, in fact, often expressed a wariness of trusting in government too much. Instead, promising that he would guarantee their safety he responded "Davy Crockett don't lie." There it is—the unadorned declaration of a frontiersman that his word is his bond, that as a man of honor he would deliver on his promises.

The success of the three Crockett episodes shocked everyone involved, but by early 1955 it had become both a popular culture and consumer phenomenon like no other. Within months merchandise associated with the new "king of the frontier" (replacing Daniel Boone for this honor) was in full production. From Crockett clothes to Crockett soap, and myriad of others (even ukuleles and face powder), no respectable American boy could be without these products. But one product above all others symbolizes the craze: the coonskin cap. While there is no evidence that Crockett ever wore such a cap, it was a logical choice from the point of view of American mythology. Ben Franklin famously wore such a cap in lieu of a powdered wig when he visited France in 1776. Franklin turned the cap into a symbol of American republicanism born out of the provincialism of American settlement—America was both primitive and advanced. Whether the boys and girls knew of the story of Franklin in Paris or not, most children would not tolerate being without this symbol of what, at the time, might be called "rugged individualism."

The merchandising of the Crockett story generated revenue exceeding $2 billion in today's dollars and would not be surpassed by even the *Star Wars* merchandising of the 1980s and 1990s. Whether Walt Disney enjoyed or even recognized the irony of the consumerist, socially conformist appeal of Crockett memorabilia, the buying craze suggested that, at least in middle- and working-class America, one struggled to express one's devotion to the principles of the inner-directed man in any way other than through symbolic purchases. Read into that fact what the chattering classes might, one thing is clear: a great number of American families believed in the virtues associated with self-reliance. If nothing else, the Davy Crockett phenomenon reveals that in the America of the 1950s the deepest American folkways remained a necessary part of our national identity.

At the heart of what we might call our crisis of national identity is a more basic question of individual identity. As we have seen, the related concerns about nation and self have been with us for three or four generations. In the years immediately after World War II Americans from scholars to day laborers confronted what we are calling the endangered self, which amounts to fears about whether a fully mature person equipped with an unshakable moral constitution still served as the model for the American citizen. Underneath this pressing concern were serious questions about whether American society and culture possessed the necessary sources of the self, the institutions that mold and equip our children, to generate future generations of Americans—persons steeped in American folkways and moral ideals.

If concern for the moral constitution of Americans was widely shared in the postwar years, the ideals for a better America were not. Most Americans admired and believed in the virtues we associate with our mythical heroes, like Davy Crockett. Many Americans still do. And while the many who so admired this American version of the "inner-directed" person worried that the forces of the world, from social conformism to globalization, were undermining our national character, a small but powerful elite have worked to transform America into something entirely new.

Dismissive of both the inner and other directed person, a new elite developed a new model of the self based on the ideals of "authenticity." The ethic of authenticity, for all its complex forms and even contradictions, has served to undermine the very institutions that have long formed the mature self. To the degree that the ideals of authenticity have been realized in policy and culture, America has become more individualistic and statist at the same time. As we will see toward the end of this book, authenticity as an ideal separates individuals from most forms of authority, especially principles of restraint drawn from religion. In place of authority, authenticity supplies abstract, universal principles the state must impose in tandem with an imperative on each individual to create a personal identity out of will and desire. Everything between the ubiquitous state and the antinomian individual is under assault.

Indeed, by our time, the healthy and morally mature person is endangered by the twin forces of statism and radical individualism. Beneath it all, however, is a deep tradition of a people, constituted by their primary institutions, and devoted to self-rule. These "unruly" people constitute not only our richest heritage but also our highest ideals. It is in defense of today's unruly Americans that we write this book about a past—our past—that constitutes the deepest and most enduring parts of our national and individual selves.

Historically, America was rooted less in a comprehensive vision of politics than an understanding of the kind of people we expected ourselves to be. It can be understood as a concern with public virtues such as honesty, hard work, fair dealing, and a combination of independent-mindedness and concern for the common good. How do we understand such virtues? Today we don't. Our forebears were taught through stories—what today are often dismissed as myths and manipulative forms of "civil religion." These stories engaged the moral imagination, they worked to convey what's needed for one to be a good person, especially in a public capacity. So, Davy Crockett's fairness, George Washington's honesty—"I cannot tell a lie, it was I who cut down the cherry tree"—and other stories and even images of heroic figures were not the equivalent of the resentful untruths of critical race theory. They were not all about politics but rather attempts to explain virtue, its nature, costs, and rewards.

In recent years, too many Americans have come to see what binds us as predominantly political in the narrow sense of simplistic, one-size-fits-all ideologies, whether of the left or the right. This, we submit, is in large measure why our politics have become so polarized and toxic. Americans are not prepared by disposition to see public life through an ideological lens or in terms of arguments over what is socially just, most efficient, or even most free in some narrow sense. Our politics historically have been rooted in the daily tasks of self-government and followed the same pattern of cooperation, competition, and low-level conflict that characterize our cultural life.

The tasks of political as well as commercial and social life are best carried out by people who know and trust one another. Aristotle wrote about the friendship of "utility" 2,500 years ago. A friendship of utility is neither selfish nor abstract but, rather, the kind of relationship an employer shares with a long-term employee, or a merchant with a regular customer, in which each trusts the other in normal circumstances to refrain from cheating and in extraordinary circumstances to try to give the other a break. The goal is to maintain the relationship for the benefit of everyone involved, not to serve any grand design.

None of this is to suggest that Americans have no coherent public philosophy—no set of habits and ideals guiding their conduct as a people. But until quite recently politics was more conversation than ideological struggle. Today we hear about the "alt-right" and the "democratic socialist" left at war with one another. Until quite recently genuinely radical views were distinctly marginalized. Our political debates were between loose coalitions of people, and more often than not impossible to define precisely in terms even of conservatism or liberalism. Why? Because they were rooted in disagreements over what practical steps were necessary for peace and prosperity in the specific circumstances of particular communities. Broader, more philosophical disagreements were few and relatively narrow because they existed within a broad consensus regarding both the priority and the nature of the common good—namely, the flourishing of our local communities. The result was not, however, either political lethargy or stultifying conformity; it was a vital, active, stunningly diverse set of communities and activities making for a dynamic as well as prosperous society. It was the resort to ideology—to abstract categories like race and class that dehumanize people and relationships—that could make politics and public life toxic.

America's Public Philosophy

Americans have no common ideology. There is no American blueprint for building the ideal society which we then try to impose on ourselves and our neighbors. Americans do, however, have a public philosophy. Until quite recently the vast majority of us accepted the importance of traditional morality, religion, hard work, political equality, consent, and especially self-government—and sought to live out these values. One might sum up this public philosophy as one of family, faith, and local freedom, provided one were careful to see each of these terms as indicating lived realities rather than mere pieties, let alone government programs. Our public philosophy flows through our veins, put there by daily interactions and the connections we have formed over the course of our lives.

Public philosophy is about public life, which is not just or even primarily about politics. A trip to the store, church, coffee shop, factory, or office takes you into the public square and is part of public life, but only in recent decades have Americans come to see the customs and rules of our interactions there as proper objects of detailed political rules. Prior to that time, and to this day for millions of Americans, politics was more about enabling than governing public life. That is, historically, Americans have looked to the central government not as a source of values or detailed standards of conduct, but rather as a tool for achieving particular, limited ends aimed at protecting our more local and fundamental communities.

Even the most radical politician still paints political programs as merely "how we do things together." But today's politics are quite the opposite of that form of interaction that once helped Americans govern themselves. Today's politics are progressive in ideology and form—they aim to transform all of society in ways that meet some uniform standard of social justice and virtue. Schools, workplaces, corporate boardrooms, and even public entertainments are to be made over, to "look like America" and "live up to our values." The claims would be true only if America were a caricature of itself in which every favored group is represented everywhere by force of law, with each of us cowed into following an ever-shifting code of conduct concerned more with virtue-signaling than protecting the associations in which people learn actual virtues. The American public philosophy had no such grand designs. It aimed, rather, to foster self-government by Americans within their local communities.

None of this is to say that American politics historically have been without conflict, any more than they were all about power, money, or any other selfish end sought by politicians or their donors. American politics always have been dynamic and filled with creative tension. But that tension was not brought about by a war of ideological visions; it was brought about by spirited discussion, by a competition among groups and impulses found within the American character. To find the sources of this discussion, and this character, we must look to what the French philosopher and observer of American life Alexis de Tocqueville called our "point of departure"—the character and tradition of the people who first settled these shores—and the development of that character through facing circumstances in history.

American Public Life before the Beginning

American public life was forged by the experience of dissenting protestants in early modern (especially sixteenth- and seventeenth-century) England. The basic elements of what would become American politics were mixed and subjected to great stress when England's prevailing, Anglican establishment sought to marginalize strict ("Puritan") protestant believers and pressure them into returning to the established Church of England. Forbidden to enter most professions and told what and to whom they could sell, where and when they could travel, and where and how they could worship, Dissenters refused to give up their faith or their way of life. In the face of government oppression, Dissenters looked inward, forging tight-knit communities in which they worked to walk together in the ways of their Lord.

Especially during the late sixteenth and early seventeenth centuries, English Dissenters established cultural and political habits deeply embedded in religious belief and practice. Dissenting communities entered into "church covenants" by which they promised God, as well as one another, to follow rules they settled among themselves according to set procedures. These covenants bound members and set down rules for governance within the community. They extended to election of civil and religious leaders as well as rules of commercial and personal conduct. Fearing English authorities and wishing to settle disputes among themselves, Dissenters set up a kind of parallel legal and constitutional structure, effectively forging civil societies within the larger kingdom.

It was this covenant model that sustained the dissenting and separatist protestants, including those who left England and played such a large role in settling the New World. It produced evocative symbols of self-government like the Mayflower Compact. It played a major role in shaping the norms (what Tocqueville called "habits of the heart") that came to dominate much of colonial life and served as a pattern for politics and culture well into the nineteenth century and, in diluted form, up to this day. The model, deeply rooted in religious practice and belief, and devoted to pursuit of the common good, was also grounded in the consent of the governed and emphasized the importance of formal rules laying out the limited authority of governing bodies. The model, tested by armed conflict, hunger, and division within isolated settlements, developed independent of the English system and into a specifically American tradition of self-government under God—a tradition that produced the American Constitution and, more important still, the American way of life.

Who Cares about the Puritans?

We aren't claiming that all or even most colonial Americans were dissenting protestants living in tight-knit, covenantal communities. The Southern and Middle colonies were populated by different peoples, ethnically, religiously, and culturally, than those in the North and produced leading figures throughout the colonial and early republican era. But the New England model was powerful and had an outsized influence on American culture and politics.

We also are not claiming that American colonists in general inhabited some golden age to which we must return, or for which we should pine. Like all human societies, English colonies in North America contained and furthered great injustices. Our point rather is that these communities embodied a way of life that in general was both good and crucial to forming our character as a society and a people. Even today we remain a nation of relative "joiners" who perceive the model of virtue presented by our traditional way of life as something to be wished for and, where possible, practiced. We can regain the national character that made possible the way of life so many Americans clearly value. But first we must understand how the genius for association at the core of our character has devolved into a life of social media, online gaming, pornography, and dating apps, interrupted by occasional bouts of political conflict.

The American way of life, like all ways of life, faced adversity from its inception. Especially important was the people's prolonged experience settling ever more territory; this experience thinned out our communities and undermined our ability to exercise our associational genius in sparsely settled areas separated from one another by vast tracts of land. The institutionalization of slavery fragmented America on sectional and racial lines in ways that remain with us to this day. And American communities experienced further stress on account of mass immigration and industrialization over the course of the nineteenth century. But, while all these circumstances undermined traditional norms, public policies did far more. Even as their communities began to lose their vitality, self-appointed leaders responded to changing circumstances by working to entrench a thin, simplified form of the public philosophy—a kind of civil religion devoted to "Americanism" that attacked key elements of actual, lived American culture, especially the variety of local, self-governed community life. Unfortunately, this program required ever-more political and cultural centralization. Accelerating after the conflagration of the Civil War, the drive to centralize power spawned crusades like the Supreme Court's drive to forge a single, "national market" by twisting the Constitution into a nationalist code barring attempts by local communities to preserve their ways of life. All this paved the way for a homegrown but mechanistic and damaging ideology called progressivism. Progressives substituted an ill-defined public will for the consent of a self-governing people within various communities, an ideology of political transformation for religious aspirations, and their own expertise for the virtuous citizenry. They set America on a path toward a cultural civil war over our way of life.

We live in the aftermath of a culture war that has cost us our public philosophy—our consensus regarding what matters most. This culture war also has cost us the strength and vitality of our most natural, important institutions—family, church, and local association. But history continues to flow, and its consequences are not permanent. Americans need not have made the many mistakes that brought us to this point. Moreover, recognizing that cultural simplification and political centralization are mistakes may help us rethink how we should approach our own problematic situation and perhaps rebuild our common life, most importantly by rebuilding our character. To do that we must relearn the fundamentals of our culture and how it can spawn a healthy politics aimed at helping self-governing communities flourish.

Norms, Culture, and the Art of Association

Many Americans would find life in a traditional community confining and even oppressive. Many more believe they would find it so, but quite possibly would not. This is because we all have grown up with caricatures and horror stories about the evils of traditional societies. Racial oppression, religious intolerance, unjust gender roles, and an overall demand for obedience to social norms. All these produced, we are told, a society in which force and fear ruled everyone's daily life.

To give pessimism its due, there is some truth to all of this, and far more truth to the recognition that we cannot simply "go back" to any supposed golden age of virtue and community. But we won't find useful guidance by starting from an idealistic vision of the "freedom" of today's public square and comparing it with the most hostile reading possible of the excesses of the past. We would be better served by examining the essentials of that earlier way of life, and especially the norms dominant then, and now.

A useful place to begin is with the public square itself—the literal public square formed by streets and buildings in the center of town, where shops, restaurants, workplaces, churches, and civic buildings exist in close proximity to one another. How do we expect ourselves as well as others to behave in these places? In times past, we would be careful to make ourselves "presentable." We would comb our hair, put on nice clothes, and make certain to watch our step and our behavior. We would make a point of acknowledging passersby and, usually, stop and chat with those we knew. We would, in a phrase, be on our best behavior because we were in public—among those whose opinions mattered to us and to whom we owed respect.

Times have changed. Today we enjoy the freedom to go out dressed however we wish—often rather undressed. Neatness is a choice, as is civility. What this means is that, for many of us, going out in public means steeling ourselves against the sights and sounds of people who feel no compunction about offending us, and may even intentionally do so. And what would offend us? In earlier times it would be people who did not abide by the social norms of the time and place. Today the same rule applies, but the norms have changed and, in many cases, ceased to operate.

For example, religious displays have been banned from most public spaces. Where they still exist, these displays are undermined and even attacked by hostile counterparts. Christmas presents the obvious case in point. Here we might consider the Satanic "Christmas" display at the Illinois Capitol and the Boca Raton public park, or the atheist "solstice" displays in Santa Monica.[3] Santa Monica's attempted solution to the problem of public expression of religious beliefs perfectly captured the new ethic. The city held an annual lottery to assign spots for holiday displays in the public park. Christmas 2018 saw a Christmas display or two, several "secular" displays disparaging religion, and a vast number of spots left vacant by groups that signed up with the sole intention of preventing religious displays. Antireligious ideologues used the "fair" procedure of random choice to strip bare their own public square. The displays were eventually banned altogether from public property.[4]

This is only one example of a paradigm shift in American public life. In part due to false readings of what is required by our Constitution and in part due to a profound weakening of the public philosophy, small groups of persons hostile to American traditions have been empowered to silence adherents to our public philosophy. We are expected to accept, if not celebrate, the new norm of often-violent dissent from community standards as public orthodoxy.

The question is whether freedom from standards of decorum and from impediments to intentionally offending passersby helps maintain a free, self-governing community. Today's freedoms themselves are quite limited; they don't include the freedom to defend traditional institutions, beliefs, and practices, or even to use "incorrect" pronouns in addressing one's fellow human beings. Still, the new norms aim at fostering a particular kind of good, namely a society of individuals who choose their own identities while imposing an ethic of public recognition and equality throughout all their political, economic, and social relations.

The new ethic of individual autonomy has proven self-contradictory, in part because it requires that the government reconfigure all our institutions to ensure that they do not "oppress" anyone through imbalances of power or by upholding traditional norms regarding things like sexual conduct. And is a community devoted to fostering maximum individual autonomy really superior to a community in which people strive to live up to customary standards, in which we reason together, over time, concerning the decency of those standards? Self-governance is not an easy form of life. It requires that we first govern our literal selves, restraining our baser impulses and subjecting ourselves to common procedures and rules. But it seems doubtful that we are well-served by the emerging standard of self-expression, in which the national government guarantees (often over the objections of more local communities) each individual's right to act as it wishes, provided that individual obeys the commands of the central authority and manages to avoid violating ever-shifting standards of "socially just" and "tolerant" conduct.

Traditional American life was life in localities. It was dominated by associations, beginning with the family and the church, but extending to commercial life, social groups, and civic organizations. We remember some of them, such as posses and the Grange, that had dramatic effects on public and political life. But the web was held together by humbler associations as well. In our age of home entertainment systems, we have trouble imagining the kinds of entertainments that grew up among a people without them. From the family sing-along to the town choral society, from the family harvest to the harvest festival, to the church social and a multitude of charitable activities, life in the American township was filled with associations. Now the functions of most of these groups have been taken over, either by the central government or by highly centralized entertainment complexes. By understanding the ways in which persons and families forged these associations we can understand who we were and who we may be again—not, to be sure, by magically eliminating modern distractions, but rather by reconnecting with the impulses toward face-to-face relationships we so clearly retain and by reforming our laws and customs to make them possible again.

It may be true that we "can't go back." But we can stop subsidizing internet-based monopolies that undermine local commerce, information sharing, and social relations. We can stop allowing local governments to impose zoning rules that make it illegal to build traditional communities. We can stop demanding that the federal government "guarantee" our well-being and so take from our communities their very reason to exist—to take care of themselves and their members according to their deeply held moral beliefs.

The Role of Contract in American Politics and Culture

A final element is necessary to understand the nature and breakdown of American society: the contract. For decades, Americans have been told that ours is a fundamentally "liberal" society. This myth of thin community and ideological thinking owes much to a misunderstanding of contracts and their role in both public and private life. The notion of society as a kind of contract, in which the people "hire" a government to tend to specific tasks and needs, goes back to medieval times. The notion became central to liberal ideology in the thought of early modern philosophers like Thomas Hobbes and John Locke, both of whom saw a kind of "social contract" at the root of political community. Before either of these philosophers wrote their important works, however, Puritan groups had developed a tradition of covenantal communities in which fellow church members entered into solemn agreements setting forth rules of commercial interaction, rule within the community, and even what we would deem private conduct.

Such covenants played a central role in the development of American public life, from the Mayflower Compact to the Constitution itself. It is no wonder, then, that most Americans see their Constitution in almost religious terms, as the basis of our common life. Sadly, this has led many to read into that document a set of ideological demands foreign to its nature and intent, as if the contract embodies all the nation's important norms and values, rather than resting upon and seeking to support them. In reality, contracts in American society always have been important, but in the specific context of a people and a set of traditions more fundamental than themselves. Like laws, contracts are highly useful, even essential social as well as economic tools. But these tools are limited in their strength and ability to transform human behavior. Only as capstones of already-existing agreements on fundamental principles can contracts, including social contracts, do their job of maintaining peace and order.

Americans have a global reputation as a commercial people. Moreover, where other peoples see business deals as part of wider webs of social interaction, Americans often see those webs—the constant "getting to know you" meetings, the exchange of gifts, and the need for costly "introductions"—as talons of corruption. Americans habitually emphasize the deal itself as not just an outgrowth but the purpose of many relationships, and this attitude leads many to think of us as a mercenary people bereft of social concerns or consciences. Perhaps this is one reason contemporary activists are so successful in browbeating American corporations into signaling their virtue by taking on progressive causes and boycotting politically incorrect business partners—too many in business believe the only way to be moral in commercial life is to serve some political end.

Traditionally, Americans looked to contracts and less formal public and private "deals" as self-contained agreements that need no outside justification. But this has not meant that we see contracts and deals in purely commercial terms, for there is more than one kind of contract. The Mayflower Compact was a special kind of contract. It quite literally formed a people who agreed to work for the common good—self-government under God—in ways that would be spelled out later, by laws they would agree on for themselves. The lesser contracts into which Americans enter for commercial dealings are not considered embodiments of social relations; instead, they rely on the social trust and shared meanings nurtured within the social contract.

Consistent with our public philosophy, Americans have shared an awareness of contracts' importance in America but emphasize different aspects of their nature. Some have emphasized contracts' grounding in communal norms and common meanings (as with the social contract among the dead, the living, and the yet unborn). Others have emphasized the role of consent and precise terms, especially in written texts. All have recognized the role of social trust in making lasting deals possible, and the grounds of this trust within the common law tradition. Both share practical and theoretical roots in the covenant tradition of dissenting Protestantism.

The contract is "liberal" in the limited sense that it emphasizes the fundamental equality of both parties to the agreement. That equality is rooted in consent—either party has the option of entering into the deal or not. In addition, the parties control the terms of the contract—because each may decline to enter, each has a voice in determining what the terms (such as the price of the goods being sold and the conditions for their delivery) are to be.

But, while the contract is generally formalized into a legal document, it rests on deeper, cultural understandings. Should there be a lawsuit over breach of the contract, the court will look to its language and take as its first and most important guide the plain meaning of the words as understood in the relevant community. Terms like "within a reasonable time," for example, often mean something very different in one industry or locality than another. As is made clear by our increasingly litigious commercial life and the increasing cost of lawyers it brings with it, cultural understandings and social trust are essential to making contracts work.

This is even more true with less formal deals. Few even realize how much business was (and still is) done in America without the need for formal contracts. A man's word genuinely can be his bond, and in face-to-face communities it had better be, or that man will find himself ostracized and perhaps bankrupted. Deals among settlers required still more social trust because it was difficult to enforce even formal contracts when so few courts were available. Moreover, deals had to be made for things quite beyond commercial trades. Towns often were built on the basis of agreements regarding which buildings would be raised first and by whom. The formalities like the goals of these deals varied widely. The point is, Americans always have made both informal deals and more formal contracts. Each rely on as they build social trust. Each is rooted in a more fundamental social contract that, in America, took a specific form.

The Mayflower Compact was far from unique in the American colonies. Succeeding communities entered into formal agreements to serve their common good. Isolated in often hostile territory, these communities forged their own governing structures and laws, over time reaching out to form alliances with one another—alliances that eventually bound colonies together while retaining substantial local self-government. These federal constitutions themselves were "deals" in that their provisions often were bargained-for compromises regarding who would govern what, and how.

Throughout the colonial era, fundamental laws were written and developed into a deep and lasting constitutional tradition. The American Constitution of 1787 was self-consciously built on top of the constitutions of thirteen states. These constitutions shared a concern to lay out the purposes of government, to situate natural rights within an understanding of man's social nature and the importance of duty toward the common good, and to set out mechanisms to limit the powers of those who govern. The federal constitution incorporated many of these elements, but in a more limited fashion and toward more limited ends—namely protection of the well-being and mutual friendships of the states and their communities. The document required technical terms and institutional provisions to protect organic communities.

The practice of covenanting and contracting within the American tradition has not been free of conflict and even tragedy. The Civil War in significant measure was fought over how to interpret our highest contract—the Constitution—and Reconstruction failed in significant measure because Americans couldn't agree on how to reestablish a functioning political "deal" given the bitterness of war and its aftermath. Unfortunately, attempts to reestablish social trust were short-circuited, in significant measure by the rise of a new conception of America. Beginning in the late nineteenth century, progressives worked to establish a new class of experts to reinterpret our common deal, in the process dismissing traditional understandings of law, contract, and constitution. Rejecting both text and customary meanings, progressives redefined the American deal as pursuit of social justice, meaning greater efficiency, political solidarity, and material equality. In place of the concrete, historical deals of the Constitution and common law they demanded a new deal, rooted in an idealized, simplified vision of man and society; they replaced social trust with dictates from the political center.

Our goal here is to show how the standards of public conduct that were a part of the American public philosophy rested on a combination of relationships and community standards that provided for real, concrete freedoms for each person, as well as for common respect and, most important, the fellow feeling and common way of life emanating from overlapping communities and interpersonal relationships. The resulting form of self-government, disordered as it may appear, was the fundamental grounding of ordered liberty.

We grew up as a settler people, existing on the boundary between the wilds of the frontier and the static self-possession of the urban core. That meant we were well-trained in the arts of association, lawmaking, and adaptation. All this put politics in the background of our lives, not least because law and government action were judged by how well they implemented the wisdom of the people as embodied in custom and a rough-and-ready form of natural law that emphasized personal honor, fair dealing, and a concrete but limited conception of the common good. Americans governed themselves through a common law mind, sure in knowledge of basic good and evil, devoted to justice as defense of people's reasonable expectations of one another, and respecting authority without bowing to any particular person, institution, or ideology.

As the American way of life came apart, more formal, legal structures not only failed to stop the decay but significantly worsened it. Why? Because too many Americans have been shaped by an ideology of individual autonomy and choice for its own sake that has been replaced in turn by a mania for using the government as a tool to force others to give one the recognition and deference one desires. Along with this ideological breakdown has come increasing hostility to the formalism and limitations of law embodied in American constitutionalism. Self-government under God through formal constitutional structures and much less formalistic, customary common law gave way to general plans of social transformation emanating from centralized governing forces anxious to bend the letter of the law to suit their own ends. The result has been further undermining of the social trust underlying our way of life. Our greatest challenge as a people lies in the fact that we are quickly becoming—may already have become—two peoples. One is shaped by and devoted to traditional American culture and its emphasis on self-government under God. The other has been so changed by progressive ideology that it rejects even progressivism in favor of a simple formula of individual autonomy—really the will to power—under the rule of a protective national government. Two such peoples cannot coexist within the same nation over time.

America's culture and character began before we became Americans. In some ways it began before any of our forebears came to these shores. It is a conversation between custom and law that has allowed for self-government, for a dynamic stability rooted in tradition, ruled by law, and dedicated to maintaining the human relationships that make life worth living. Americans increasingly are strangers to one another, joined only by pastimes, recreational interests, and political alliances. No free government can last among a people so distanced from one another; those who rule will either cease to rule or become rulers in a more authoritarian sense, making Americans subjects rather than citizens. But this is something new in our history—something destructive and unnatural within our culture, and something that we can and should stop and reverse. To do this we must remember the way of life that our forebears bequeathed to us with the understanding that we would pass it down to our descendants.

NOTES

1. David Riesman, Nathan Glazer, and Reuel Denny, *The Lonely Crowd: A Study of the Changing American Character* (New York: Doubleday Anchor: 1953). Riesman was one of three authors, though the other two, Nathan Glazer and Ruel Denny, are largely neglected in the discussion of this book.

2. Wilfred M. McClay, "The Strange Career of *The Lonely Crowd,*" in Thomas L. Haskell and Richard F. Teichgraeber III, eds. *The Culture of the Market* (Cambridge University Press, 1996), 414.

3. Dom Calicchio, "Satanic display inside Illinois Statehouse days before Christmas draws protesters," *New York Post*, last modified December 23, 2021, accessed June 9, 2022, https://nypost.com/2021/12/23/satanic-display-inside-illinois -statehouse-days-before-christmas-draws-protesters/ https://wsvn.com/news/local/ satanic-display-included-in-boca-raton-holiday-parade/. Patrick Healy and Daisy Lin, "Atheist Display Space Puts Squeeze on Santa Monica Nativity Scenes," NBC Los Angeles, last modified December 10, 2011, accessed June 9, 2022, https://www .nbclosangeles.com/news/local/traditional-nativity-scenes-outnumbered-by-atheist -displays-in-santa-monica/1913885/.

4. Michael Allen, "No Christmas Display in Santa Monica, First Time in 60 Years," *Opposing Views*, last modified March 1, 2018, accessed June 9, 2022, https: //www.opposingviews.com/religion/churches-sue-christmas-displays-santa-monica -california. The Christmas displays were eventually moved to private church property: Fabian Lewkowicz, "Santa Monica Christmas Nativity Scene," *Santa Monica Closeup*, December 23, 2018, accessed June 9, 2022, http://www.santamonicacloseup .com/home/2018/12/23/santa-monica-christmas-nativity-scene.html.

Chapter 1

Unruly Pilgrims

1620, off the coast of Cape Cod:

William Bradford had a discipline problem. This was somewhat ironic, given that many considered Bradford himself to be a discipline problem. A leader of what we today call the Pilgrims, he and his brethren referred to themselves as Saints—a name that said a great deal about their willingness to set high standards for themselves. Sometimes referred to as Separatists, they were the most extreme protestant dissenters from the established Church of England, believing that the Anglican church was beyond redemption. Unlike the Puritans, the Pilgrims insisted on forming separate churches where their own strict Calvinism might rule.

In response to their nonconformity, the authorities of the Anglican church and the King's government subjected the Separatists to spying, threats, fines, and imprisonment. The persecution was so great they formed secret churches—tight-knit communities of believers—for their own safety and consciences. At the turn of the seventeenth century, a group of them fled to Holland. Appalled, however, by Holland's lax morals, a number of them struck a bargain with the English establishment and set off for the New World and the opportunity to govern themselves. There they would settle within the colony of Virginia—but not too close to the settlement at Jamestown, where adventurers' sinful practices might endanger the Saints' way of life.

Unfortunately, the winds had blown Bradford's people hundreds of miles off course. Low on provisions as winter set in, they would have to disembark where they were. Here was the source of the discipline problem. Separatism could only go so far. The Saints, mostly merchants and professionals, had been forced to bring along various craftsmen and servants—whom they called "Strangers" because they were not members of the Saints' congregation—who had skills necessary for their mission's success. The mission: to found a community in which Saints might walk together in the ways of their

23

Lord beyond the meddling control of hostile elites and distant from the sinful seductions of strangers.

Strangers outnumbered Saints on the *Mayflower*. And the Strangers were making noises about being free to rule themselves because they were outside the lands of Virginia, and, therefore, beyond the reach of law. For now, ship's discipline was holding, but it would not apply on land. A way must be found to bind Saints and Strangers together, lest the mission fail, and all 102 settlers perish in this inhospitable land.

Bradford was not without resources. In addition to the ship's crew, he could call on the Separatists' long tradition of forging communities. Their church covenants had bound local congregants to one another for over one hundred years. In these covenants they had promised God and one another to follow rules they settled among themselves. The rules governed election of civil and religious leaders as well as commercial and personal conduct. Fearing the authorities and wishing to settle disputes among themselves, Separatists in England had set up parallel legal and constitutional structures, effectively forging civil societies within the larger kingdom.

It would be decades before Thomas Hobbes would write of society as a contract and even longer before John Locke espoused the modern liberal theory that governments are creatures of the people who form them through voluntary agreements. But Bradford, following tradition, helped put together a "compact" that forged a self-ruling community in the wilderness, rooted in equality before God and committing both signers and nonsigners (including women, children, and several Strangers) to abide by rules and procedures the community would make for itself.

The document Bradford wrote down (we don't know how much of it he composed himself) followed well-established forms, adapted to new circumstances. It began "in the name of God" because God was both witness and party to it. It declared the group's loyalty to their King and their determination to serve God and country. It announced the signers' intention to "Combine ourselves together in a Civil Body Politic for our better ordering." It then bound them all to frame and follow "just and equal laws," offices, and procedures to serve the common good.[1]

The document was, of course, the Mayflower Compact, and its importance, like that of the Pilgrims themselves, has been much debated. Plymouth colony barely survived its first winter in the New World and soon became just one among many small communities in New England. But the compact and the people who formed it both embodied and inspired a way of life and an approach to politics central to the American tradition. The American habit of bringing order through voluntary agreement (contract, compact, covenant, or constitution) was a product of experience well before it became a cherished ideal. This habit did not depend on any theory of the state of nature or any claims about individual rights. It was a habit born from the need to bring about order.

The Mayflower Compact was a legal document in the sense that it bound the parties who signed it, in the sight of God, in the sight of one another, and in the crucial sense that it was taken by the signatories as consent to abide by (and potentially be punished under) rules laid out under its authority. To call it a "social contract" is not necessarily incorrect, but it risks imposing individualistic ideas of consent from a later period on these devoutly religious and communitarian people. It was, however, an agreement—a kind of contract—to live together, abiding by common rules and, perhaps most important, to pursue the common good as understood within the Calvinist tradition the people brought with them to the New World.

Colonists who came to New England after Bradford's Pilgrims literally followed their example by forging tight-knit religious communities. They also followed the Pilgrims by using the church covenant as a model for self-government. More generally, American colonies shared Plymouth's commitment to adopting "Puritanical" rules of behavior. Most of these restrictions (from prohibitions against adultery to punishment for failing to attend church) were common in England as well, but less often, less vigorously, and less equally enforced in that populous, aristocratic, and loose-knit kingdom. Even Virginia sternly enforced and vigorously punished everything from failure to attend religious services to theft and idleness, though more explicitly in the interests of survival.

New England's Puritan communities differed from those in other areas because of their strict Calvinist beliefs and ongoing conflicts over these beliefs. These were, after all, unruly Pilgrims, committed to their own faith and to embodying that faith in functioning communities against the demands for conformity by church and government authorities. Claims to special knowledge and calls to saintly perfection abounded, even spawning occasional rash social experiments (coming to the New World itself had been a rash experiment). But extremism was mostly kept in check by local authorities and the favored (though not sole) punishment for those who caused too much trouble was banishment, not death. Other colonies to the south also sometimes punished dissenters, who seemed to crop up no matter what the official religion of any specific community.

As we will explore in the coming chapters, cultures and political practices varied significantly among English colonies in North America. That rich pluralism became a very important part of the American story of self-rule. From its beginnings, and from before its beginnings, America was a nation of unruly Pilgrims, seeking wealth, adventure, but most especially a way of life embodied in local communities. They worked hard, took their faith seriously, and were willing to fight to maintain their way of life—including against one another. Cooperation was essential to survival, as competition for status and success was to be welcomed, and conflict was natural in the struggle for survival and self-government. Conflicts abounded in the New World. But the first great conflict would take 150 years to ripen and would involve American communities' determination to conserve their traditions of self-government.

NOTES

1. "The Mayflower Compact," in Bruce Frohnen, ed., *The American Republic: Primary Sources,* (Indianapolis: Liberty Fund, 2002), 11.

Chapter 2

The Roots of American Culture

American self-understanding is, and long has been, deeply distorted by two things. First, our collective understanding of our history, however variable among groups and partisans, is inadequate, even wrong.[1] Second, we Americans are often trapped within a political, social, and cultural vocabulary that distorts historical reality and the motives behind our own actions. In short, we have the wrong map of our national reality, and so we almost never end up where we want. Through history rather than ideological labels we hope to supply a better map that shows us where we have been and therefore how to find our way to a better America, a better us.

Most books today that offer road maps to national consensus, political and social harmony, or even to partisan victory at the polls, depend on very recent developments (demographic data, changing attitudes as reported in polls, and so forth) and pay scant attention to deeper historical currents. However, the past has much greater power over us than the authors of these books realize, and understanding contemporary crises properly must include a reliable and useful history.

Going back to the roots of American culture[2] forces us to confront some important truths about America. First, as a matter of historical fact, settlers were more important to creating our culture than immigrants. Scholars in the 1960s and 70s—particularly in the field of Cultural Geography—concluded that those who first occupy a territory or who take the land by pushing others off, have an enormous impact on the region's culture for centuries. The power of settlers—often a miniscule population compared to later waves of immigrants—is enormous; establishing linguistic patterns, religious beliefs, architectural and other material cultural traits, marriage and family structures, and a host of other folkways. Among these are beliefs or ideas, which will be our primary focus. But ideas are not necessarily more important than sports, food, clothing, dialect, or class. All of these are bound together. The constellation of ways of living, beliefs, cultural ideals, and aspirations supply the culture into which immigrants come. These immigrants typically become participants in this host culture, altering it in important ways without destroying it. After all, aside from the slaves whose cultural impact we discuss later, immigrants *chose* to come to a particular place and had to "get on" within a particular community, even if they sought also to maintain and even spread their own traditions. From a historically distant perspective, continuities stand out much more than changes.

An example of the lasting importance of settlers on emerging cultural forms is New Amsterdam and the curiosity that became New York City. In 1624, before the Puritans founded the Massachusetts Bay Colony, the Dutch settled a tiny outpost that would eventually become the world's most influential city. It is safe to say that the New York City of today would not exist had it not been for the fact that the Dutch were there first. Between 1624 and their conquest by the British in 1664—a scant forty years—the tiny Dutch settlements in and around Fort Amsterdam (including the villages of "Haarlem," "Breukelen," "Staaten Eylandt" and "Hoboken") established a culture that would give New York City a character unlike any other city—a character that would be important in the late-eighteenth-century negotiations about a national government. Being in a cultural minority, the citizens of New York City would only join a national union if they could protect their independence.

In the seventeenth century the Netherlands was the most powerful commercial nation in the world. The global reach of this small nation, and its focus on commerce, made the Dutch prize tolerance highly because it was a necessary condition for engaging in such a diverse world of trading partners. As Colin Woodard puts it, "they didn't celebrate diversity but tolerated it, because the alternative was far worse."[3] New Amsterdam was initially controlled by a corporation (the Dutch West India Company) which was interested exclusively in trade (initially trade for fur pelts acquired from the interior). Focused on commerce, with no religious purpose or even any serious interest in crafting a cohesive community, the Dutch created the most diverse city in the New World (including at least one Muslim, French-speaking Walloons, Poles, Finns, Irish, Portuguese, and Africans, to name a few). By the time the British took over, New Amsterdam was a rather wild mix of ethnicities, religions, and languages with all this diversity organized for the purpose of trade and commerce. The small outpost quickly became the center for trade in all manner of things, from fur pelts and tobacco to New England cod and a variety of manufactured goods.

As one might expect of such a commercial town perched at the edge of a great "wilderness," opportunities to succeed or fail were open to those with daring. The elite that emerged in this city was composed of self-made men who championed entrepreneurialism while deemphasizing any moralism that got in the way of trading and profit-making. These characteristics would be very important much later on the issue of slavery and the hugely profitable cotton industry.

New York City is an excellent example of the persistence of character traits and folkways long after the small number of early settlers had been swamped by immigrants. But New York City's non-British origins notwithstanding, the America that emerged as a nation was overwhelmingly the product of British cultures. Therefore, to understand America today we must understand its tangled cultural origins, which are prior to, and more lasting than, political, constitutional, or social developments. In fact, the institutions, as well as the political and constitutional arrangements that define the American "founding" were the results of an amazingly complex cultural pluralism that gave national "unity" a particular character that persists to this day. Any hope of a sustainable American unity going forward rests on cultural pluralism strong enough to withstand the eroding character of contemporary globalism and an alluring but false "nationalism" based on abstract principles. As we will make clear, Americans are an unruly, contentious people who negotiate our way to unity while retaining our multiple sources of cultural vitality. "Transformation" is the ideal of ideologues who want to eradicate our tangled, messy roots in favor of a clean, pure, and easily managed political and social order.

The American order was neither clean nor easily managed. This is a good thing, as we hope to show. To sort out this historical messiness and to demonstrate the importance to our national culture of our unruly nature, we draw on one of the great, now classic, works of early American history, David Hackett Fischer's *Albion's Seed: Four British Folkways in America*. Anyone wanting to understand this subject in greater depth and detail would be well advised to begin with Fischer's exhaustive and well-researched book. We can only summarize and highlight key themes, augmenting with newer scholarship.

Some very powerful elements of a common American culture were present from early in the colonial experience. First, colonial Americans largely shared English as a common language. English was not universally the first language of colonial inhabitants—particularly in Pennsylvania, which included a great variety of non-English speakers—but it was nonetheless the language of British America in government, commerce, and most of civil society. What is more important, perhaps, is that dialects varied dramatically by region, often to the point of making communication challenging.

Second, the vast majority of colonials were protestant, the largest but not the only exception being the Roman Catholics of Maryland. Like the English language, Protestantism came in widely varying and utterly incompatible forms and so American Protestantism produced a common ground of beliefs and values for American culture while also creating tensions and arguments that required national compromises to secure regional or local difference. Tolerance was a practical necessity rather than an imposed ideal.

Third, Americans lived under and generally admired British law and the common law that underwrote it. A widely perceived belief among colonials in the 1770s that the British government was acting unlawfully and—to antici-pate the next point—threatening the liberties of colonials, was a key reason why a reasonably organized rebellion was possible for these diverse people.

Fourth, the colonials shared a strong attachment to British liberties. Liberty meant many different things to colonial Americans—and those differences matter a great deal to our story—but they all held dear inherited liberties as their rightful bequests from ancestors.

Whether these areas of commonality were greater than the myriad of dif-ferences is not as important as most people assume once we understand that American culture—the common ground that made nationhood possible—depended just as much on the depth and nature of American pluralism as it did on these four shared cultural traits. It is one of the wonders of America that we have crafted and continue to craft a nation that respects our unruly nature and our need to belong to different and varying cultures.

The roots of American culture, then, are found in at least four distinct "folk-ways"[4] or cultures, each in turn rooted in a distinct region of Britain. The first "wave" of settlers was concentrated between 1629 and 1640 when Puritans from the East Anglia region of England very purposely planted a very particu-lar, even eccentric, English subculture in Massachusetts. This migration took place as Charles I ruled without—or against—Parliament and in violation of developed English liberties and prerogatives. More importantly, Charles fought with elements within the Anglican Church as he moved to consoli-date his power and to force greater uniformity in the church in opposition to Puritans and other groups. As the English Puritans organized and carried out the settling of Massachusetts, the struggle over church doctrine and political power was foremost on their minds and the primary reason for their efforts. For decades after the issues that created the conflict in England had faded away, Puritan New England remained obsessed with them.

Whether an "escape to the wilderness" or a second front in the war over the soul of the Anglican Church, the Puritans came with amazing singleness of mind. Rejecting religious tolerance,[5] this cohort of migrants was strikingly homogeneous. Not only did most of the first generation of settlers share reli-gious convictions, educational background, professional similarities, family structure, and purpose for migrating, but they severely restricted subsequent immigration to favor those like themselves. Such collective singleness of mind was essential to their goal of establishing and maintaining a haven for Puritanism that allowed for the full implementation of their ideas of church, state, and society.

At the core of their ideals was self-rule. To this end New Englanders planted new towns as groups who migrated together. Having made a covenant with each other to worship together and to watch over each other as they sought to live godly lives, they understood their towns to be extensions of their contractual duties to be their neighbor's keeper.

These towns would be governed by the local citizens who, as much as possible, made decisions collectively and by consensus. Dissenters to the governing ethos of each town were dangerous to the integrity of this self-governing body and so these communities regularly purged (often informally rather than by law) those who didn't fit in. At the same time, being Englishmen who had experienced political tyranny in the form of King Charles, the Puritans were devoted to both inherited English liberties and to English legal traditions that limited power. The Puritan way of thinking about power was to contrast public power—the power of the community collectively—with the power expressed by individual persons. The goal of the town was ultimately the "public good" and tyranny always came as a challenge to the public or collective good.

Puritans' passionate devotion to local and popular rule (what Alexis de Tocqueville later called "township freedom") had the effect of producing a species of distributive freedom; distributing the freedom to rule their towns as they saw fit required that they allow other towns to do the same, whether they approved of their choices or not. The only system by which a people could govern themselves this fully, in such detailed ways, and with stern judgment against those who disagreed was one that produced many competing but intolerant towns. A pluralism of intolerance turned out to be one of the keys to American freedom, broadly understood.

These Puritan origins fostered in New England a culture devoted to strong communities bound by conscious (and contractually defined) purpose, dedicated to the public good, emphasizing public services to support the weakest members of the community, and producing a culture of morally judgmental busybodies. Over time, as Puritans became Yankees, these traits persisted, eventually in more secular forms. Puritan or Yankee culture would not just thrive in New England but be planted further west, from portions of the Midwest to Oregon—a lateral band of Yankeedom that would never have existed had the first settlers not been Puritans.

The cultural divide between Yankeedom and the Virginia settlement could hardly have been sharper given their common English heritage. This "second wave" of settlement took place primarily between 1649 and 1660 from a "broad band of territory that extended from Kent and Devon north to Northamptonshire and Warwickshire."[6] Not only did the leadership—the governing class—of Virginia come from a different region of England than the Puritans, they also came from a different class and with different goals.

The Interregnum in England—the period between the execution of King Charles I and the restoration of the monarchy with Charles II—was a period of Puritan persecution of the defeated royalists. Many of these royalists, typically younger sons of aristocrats, migrated to Virginia with the objective of replicating a hierarchical system of rule based on fixed classes and an agricultural economy. Seeking to restore their way of life, these "cavaliers" also stressed a high Anglicanism quite hostile to Puritans and other dissenting groups and a set of cultural traits associated with feudal societies, honor and military virtues being the most important.

As tobacco emerged as a profitable crop capable of creating great wealth to sustain oligarchic rule, Virginian planters sought new sources of labor to maximize their advantages. The early dependence on indentured servants (mainly English, but some African) quickly created a two-tiered system of Englishmen that would replicate itself through the American revolution. No former servant nor son of a former servant ever served in the colonial legislature. That sort of mobility was almost impossible in this place and time. What began as a strict class system turned, over time, into race-based slavery of the sort already in practice in the Caribbean and South America, to solve the pressing need for labor. As a result, by the early eighteenth century Virginia produced a three-tiered order that included an oligarchic elite, poor white citizens, and enslaved Africans and their offspring.

Coming at different times, from different English cultures, and with different purposes, Massachusetts and Virginia produced economic, social, and cultural orders that were necessarily incompatible and therefore hostile. No less dramatic was the contrasting nature of the third migration, from 1675 to 1715, led by Quakers. In just a few decades the number of Quakers in the colonies made them the third-largest denomination in British America, a dramatically higher percentage of the population than today, when they are the sixty-sixth-largest denomination.

Like the Puritans, the Quakers came to America for religious reasons. Persecution in England was often severe (as it was in both Puritan and Anglican colonies in America), but it was only partially about escape from persecution and more of a desire to demonstrate what a society governed by Quaker principles would look like. Settling in the Delaware Valley, with the largest concentration in Pennsylvania, the Quakers designed a society and government that took tolerance and religious freedom as its cornerstone. Unlike other colonies, Pennsylvania actively encouraged immigration from non-English people and from members of different churches. As a result, thousands of Germans and other Europeans, mostly from pietistic Christian sects, settled in Pennsylvania.

Far from being a more secular region of the colonies, as some suggest, Pennsylvania's rich combination of Christian piety and religious diversity (in doctrine and practice) produced a morally earnest yet tolerant society that persisted long after the original motivations for migration had faded away. These characteristics endeared them to neither the Puritans to the north nor the Cavaliers to the South, and so the introduction of a Quaker culture to British North America created yet more suspicion among the different cultures and regions.

The least powerful wave of settlers but perhaps the most influential in the long run was the borderland migration. This fourth wave was the longest in duration, from 1717 to 1775, and was by far the largest, bringing over 250,000 people. Ethnically diverse (Scottish, English, Irish, among others) and divided by religion—Presbyterians and Anglicans being the vast majority—these migrants were what Fischer calls Borderlanders, though in America we have typically lumped them under the category "Scotch-Irish," which implies an ethnic homogeneity that didn't exist. These immigrants did not come for religious reasons and had no visions about an ideal society; the Borderlanders cared little for the idea of tolerance and they possessed no privilege to protect. They were unlike the other settlers in almost every respect.

Borderlanders were, in many respects, refugees. For 800 years, the borderland area between England and Scotland had been fought over by nations when it wasn't simply a government-less region. Constant conflict and resulting violence, often less a war and more the chaos of anarchy, marked this region's peoples much more than ethnicity or religion. These peoples shared deep cultural similarities born of profound insecurity and constant, capricious death.

Among the deepest cultural traits Borderlanders brought with them to America were a deep suspicion of governmental power and of distant elites, a tendency to prefer individual liberty over communal goods, an aversion to towns in favor of "hermitages," and deep loyalty to clan (rather than the nuclear family), which served as the primary institution governing their lives. Constant violence and warfare not only caused Borderlanders to prefer the virtues of the warrior over those of the merchant, but encouraged frequent migration. As a result, they cared relatively little for fixed property (which can be destroyed without much warning). The lawlessness that featured so prominently in their history caused them to take law and order into their own hands and to embrace a very powerful system of honor and shame as the best way of enforcing norms and bringing some order.

Like the Puritans of New England, but in a profoundly different way, the Borderlanders were devoted to the idea of self-rule. They had long developed cultural traits to take care of themselves in the midst of chaos or impending chaos and they had cultivated norms appropriate to people who must fend for themselves, who cannot trust strangers, and who live mostly in the present.

Those who came to America were often the most desperate or the most adventuresome of this population, and when they arrived, typically in Philadelphia, they often hightailed it to the backwoods of Pennsylvania and Virginia, where there was little or no government control and where they could continue their long-standing tradition of fighting over land, this time with warrior peoples like the Shawnee, and then, later, the Cherokee, Creek, Choctaw, and Chickasaw. Moving frequently, often away from settled areas (with some important exceptions) these settlers eventually occupied the Appalachian region and over the next century their cultural dominance spread to Arkansas, Missouri, Texas, and later Oklahoma. As a culture they controlled an area the size of Europe. But their cultural reach was even broader than that as descendants would be deeply influential in the Southwest as well, and particularly in Southern California. The American species of "individualism" and, especially, self-reliance, springs largely from the culture of these Borderlanders.

The vast majority were poor when they migrated to America, but they were almost all skilled workers and their motivations were more or less universal—the pursuit of a better life, more opportunity, and the freedom to live on their own terms. The contrast between these new immigrants who disembarked in Philadelphia and the Quaker dominated culture of that region could hardly have been sharper: pacifist vs warrior, communal good vs individual liberty, cosmopolitanism vs a proud provincialism. Indeed, the Borderlanders' combination of poverty and intense personal pride was not only grating on the Quaker majority but downright befuddling—a characteristic, as much as any other, that would characterize the borderland people throughout much of American history.

These four cultural folkways (Puritan/Yankee, Cavalier/Southern, Quaker/midlands, and Borderlander) proved astonishingly resilient and, with the exception of the Cavalier, also quite good at planting versions of themselves farther west, further reinforcing these four cultures as American from coast to coast. But they were also incompatible with each other, creating all manner of conflict and, when cooperation was necessary, requiring that Americans forge agreements by way of contracts and constitutions that limited the scope of cooperation in such a way as to protect the independence of each culture.

These four major folkways, along with New Amsterdam, constitute the roots of American culture. But there is another, a fifth and malignant culture, that we will address in the next chapter. We can neither understand the nature and purpose of the founding nor the American character that has emerged in the centuries since without coming to grips with this peculiar cultural pluralism, with the conflict that has always been part of the American political union, and with the moral contradictions that have played such a central role in our self-understanding, our national identity.

NOTES

1. Excellent histories abound of the United States and a significant number of Americans have a deep understanding of American history. We are here talking about historical narratives and themes that dominate our public understanding of our nation. The historical distortions are not necessarily greater among the less educated since some of the most dangerous misunderstandings of our history (and by extension the answer to the question: who are we?) are among our elite in media, academia, and high-tech industries, among others.

2. The roots of American culture are more than complicated—they are messy and not fully visible even to the best scholars. Russell Kirk wrote one of the most important books on this subject, *The Roots of the American Order* (Wilmington, DE: ISI, 2003). His focus was on the ordering principles at the heart of American culture and the roots he found went back to the Ancient Israelites, among others. We recommend this book strongly, but our goal is more focused: to find the sources of an American culture out of its British folkways.

3. Colin Woodard, *American Nations: A History of the Eleven Rival Regional Cultures in North America* (New York: Penguin, 2012), 70. Woodard's book builds on Fischer's work but adds more regional complexity and diversity. His discussion of New Amsterdam, from which this section is drawn, is a valuable addition to understanding American cultural pluralism, then and now.

4. Folkways are both deeper and less intellectualized than much of what scholars take as culture. Habits of settlement (whether in towns, clusters of homes, or isolated homesteads), child-rearing, and treatment of the bodies of deceased members of the community all help make up a people's way of life and influence attitudes and behaviors toward strangers, business partners, and members of any common political unit. See especially David Hackett Fischer, *Albion's Seed: Four British Folkways in America* (New York: Oxford, 1996).

5. Among the most distorting claims about this story is that the Puritans came in search of religious freedom. Such historical nonsense has prevented several generations from understanding the conflictual nature of American unity and the special quality to the American species of toleration. Toleration is something we value as a practical response to a certain kind of pluralism, and this toleration does not aim to undermine profound differences but to highlight them, give differences the freedom to mature and fructify.

6. Fischer, *Albion's Seed*, 786. Of course, settlement began well before 1649, but Fischer's argument about "waves" focuses on when sufficient numbers began settling the region and creating a cultural imprint.

Chapter 3

Slavery

The history we want is never the history we've got. This is a good thing even as it is a universal truth of humankind. The yearning for a clean, unblemished history is natural, because we cannot fully separate ourselves from our past, and so our past will own us if we don't learn to own it. We are not who we are without the remembered past (history) and, to a degree that we rarely recognize, the unremembered past, which lives with us in the forms of assumptions, cultural habits, linguistic patterns, and all manner of persistent traits that we rarely examine. Truth telling about our past is not only a moral obligation but also a way of understanding ourselves. Truthful history helps us not be hostage to powerful but hidden cultural currents and preserves us from the dangerous seduction of ideology that invites us to live in the abstract purity of a future dream. While we like things to be clean and simple, we need to learn that this desire poses greater danger than embracing a messy and complicated history.

In America, the most troubling part of our history concerns slavery and a persistent legacy of racism, and here too the roots well predate nationhood. The four folkways that David Hackett Fischer explored so brilliantly in *Albion's Seed*, and which were the subject of the previous chapter, are each complex and none perfect. Nor are they equal in virtue, for no two cultures are ever really equal. But a fifth culture—one that Fischer incorporated into his analysis of the Cavaliers and their founding in the Chesapeake—warrants a separate examination. This fifth British culture or folkway is the geographically and numerically limited but politically dominant ruling class of the Deep South, and this story begins in Barbados.

By the mid seventeenth century, the small island of Barbados was, as Colin Woodard so aptly put it, "the richest and most horrifying society in the English-speaking world." The majority of settlers before 1640 were British indentured servants who acquired land after their period of indenture. In great need of laborers, wealthy plantation owners imported Scottish and Irish prisoners (captured in war) and even kidnapped children, putting them to work under horrific conditions. The introduction of sugarcane from Dutch Brazil in 1640 created the most lucrative export for the island and the need for a much larger and more reliable labor source. The Dutch, at first, supplied the English plantations of Barbados with financing, access to European markets, and African slaves. Almost immediately Barbados was turned into a slave society, creating a brutal slave code (which would be the model for slave colonies in America) that was part of a system of exploitation known far and wide for its shocking level of dehumanization.

In 1670, second and third sons of Barbadian plantation owners, looking to extend their lucrative plantation system, landed at what would become Charleston, South Carolina. "The society they founded in Charleston," explains Woodard, in contrast to Virginia and the other colonial settlements, "did not seek to replicate rural English manor life or to create a religious utopia in the American wilderness. Instead, it was a near-carbon copy of the West Indian slave state these Barbadians had left behind, a place notorious even then for its inhumanity."

The founding Charter of "Carolina" (formally separated into two colonies in 1712) written by John Locke in 1663, while Charles II was king, reflected the interests of West Indies planters. Among the provisions was the grant to upper-class settlers of 150 acres for every servant or slave brought to the colony, making it possible for a few Barbadian planters to own the best land in a matter of a few years. And so, like the Cavaliers who settled Virginia, these English planters established a deeply hierarchical social system, a rural economy (though with an urban center where most of the richest lived, Charleston) based on cash crops requiring intensive labor.

Other similarities are important as well. At least at a superficial level, the Barbadian landholders held the same political views as the Virginian Cavaliers. Both were Royalists and had fought—or in the case of those in Barbados, ancestors and relatives had fought—on the losing side in the English Civil War and both were pleased at the return of the king in 1660 in the form of Charles II. It was after Charles that they named Charles Town, which became Charleston. Both sets of elites were supporters of the Anglican church, though the planters in Carolina were conspicuously less religious. And finally, while Virginia (and the entire tidewater region) became a slave society, Carolina was founded as one.

The differences between these two colonial cultures look subtle to modern eyes but were profound to seventeenth- and eighteenth-century colonials. The early elites of Virginia wanted to establish a class system, not a racist social order. A rich and mature historical literature traces the evolution of a racist system that led, in the second and third generations, to adopting a version of chattel slavery already practiced in the West Indies and South America. As we note in our previous book, slavery was not a part of the English tradition or laws and was proscribed by English common law. Its evolution in Virginia was possible only because of the loose nature of British control over the colonies along with Parliament's decision to allow, in what amounts to an innovation with profound implications, local positive law abrogating long-standing common law. In Virginia, the development of race-based slavery (or any slavery) was a rejection of their English roots, though, as we will explore, part of the roots of the American regime.

But in Virginia the limits of slavery were also evident in the colonial period. A large population of Borderlanders who didn't seek to participate in this slave society and whose growing numbers prevented the westward spread of Virginia's culture along with a deep ambiguity about slavery, produced a strange cultural mix. Out of this mix came Thomas Jefferson, whose land was in the Piedmont area, not far from the libertarianism of the Borderlander population. He and other elites of this region sought an escape from this slave system even as they developed or promulgated ideas of natural rights and equality that would become the most electric political ideas of the next two centuries.

The slave society founded in Carolina had little of this ambiguity. A thoroughly racist belief system, wrought from their experiences as beneficiaries of extreme wealth amid horrific slavery in Barbados, was integral to the settlers' culture. Indeed, what today we would call genetic differences were central to Carolinian elites' beliefs; they celebrated their own Norman bloodlines in contrast to the Saxon majority of both England and America. This claim to ethnic superiority would not only create conflict with the Borderlanders who lived on the edges of their territory but frame their attitude toward most English settlers to America, with particular distaste for the people and society of New England.

The fifth culture would not only settle into the Carolinas but expand to what we now call the Deep South. In the case of Georgia, which was founded as a non-slave colony for English poor people to become self-sufficient landholders, Carolina's elite, seeking to further expand their profitable plantation system, quickly overwhelmed the original settlers and altered its character and charter. By the late colonial period, the elite of this slave society were among the wealthiest Americans and had power greater than their numbers would suggest. After the revolution, their power grew dramatically as they established cotton plantations across Alabama, Mississippi, Louisiana, and Arkansas, as well as parts of other states. In all of these states they replicated the racist society they first established in South Carolina and, as their wealth and power grew, became the dominant voice of the South. In contrast, the Virginia that produced the great leaders of the American revolution and defended with ardor second to none the liberty and the natural rights of every human, became ever weaker politically and more or less hemmed in geographically because of the growing influence of the Borderlander culture in the western part of the state.

Borderlanders would settle in the Western mountains of Carolina and Georgia but would never achieve the political or cultural relevance they exercised in Virginia. They were isolated socially and geographically from circles of power throughout the Deep South and found themselves ruled against their will by elites whom they detested. Their alienation would produce often-overlooked conflicts during the Revolutionary and Civil Wars with reverberations to this day.

Slave society, and the culture it supported, would become the greatest threat to both the American Republic and the "empire of liberty" that functioned as the central element of American character. We will turn to liberty—or liberties—and the nature of the American regime in the next chapter and explore how this land of different, unruly, and fractious cultures produced something common and shared. The hardest part of that story to understand is the role played by slave societies. America was hardly exceptional in this regard because slavery was so widespread and had been a key part of human life throughout history. But what is exceptional—or at least deeply troubling—about the American version of this shameful aspect of human history is how closely coupled liberty and slavery were and how decoupling them has proven to be the tragic fate of those generations that have followed.

In this book we celebrate America's heritage and we embrace the traditions and folkways that have the longest history in the experiences of free peoples going back long before any Englishmen came to America. But like all great stories worth celebrating, it comes with not only its sins and evils, but with a deep sadness that is part of our inheritance.[1] The challenge to embrace a heritage that includes such evil and still engenders so much sadness is the same one facing every culture, every civilization, every nation. One of the great opportunities that comes from historical truth telling is to understand our heritage in a way that engenders gratitude, a real and profound sense of humility at the limits of any generation of people, and the kind of humble knowledge that spurs the great work of civilization: preserving, pruning, and improving.

NOTES

1. One of the most brilliant analyses of this sad legacy is Paul Conkin's essay, "Hot, Humid and Sad," where he ends with the complexity of this sadness, tied to guilt among the guiltless descendants, the stigma that they cannot shake, and with a powerful explanation of the way the past shapes and even traps us. It is worth quoting at some length.

"The burden of this past rests most heavily on blacks, but not much less so than on poor, economically insecure whites. Blacks are doubly victims, of racial bias and a bias against southern culture with its complicated mixture of British and African roots. And no easy or early answers are possible for blacks. They were servile, then low caste, and even now, when legally liberated, still without the secure historical tradition and self-worth that typifies those southern whites who formerly monopolized knowledge, ownership, and power. For some blacks, insecurity has propelled them into a competitive frenzy, as the middle class moves rapidly to equality in income and wealth. For others it has meant frustration, alienation, and all types of pathology, in crime, family decay, and poverty. . . . This is tragic, in the most literal sense. Southerners are in a trap, created by past choices, and without any early way out."

As the essay ends, Conkin asks a series of questions that, over twenty-five years later, seem even more pressing. "How many years, how many generations, will it take southerners to escape the ego-shattering fallout from their past? How much achievement, even compensatory overachievement, will finally allow southerners, black and white, wherever they now live, to relax and accept as normal what is now so much more open to them than ever before—economic opportunity, cultural attainment, and, above all, moral complacency? How soon can acknowledged guilt bestow on former oppressors a sense of forgiveness? How soon can the past suffering of victims eventuate in some measure of redemption? How soon? (Paul K. Conkin, *A Requiem for the American Village* [Lanham, MD: Rowman & Littlefield, 2000], 174).

Chapter 4

A Plural Nation

American Liberties and the Birth of a People

The name of our nation, "The United States of America," reveals a great deal about our origins and about the character of our country. We began as a nation of states, not as a nation with states. However, as our previous chapters reveal, the colonies and then states were really not as important as the cultural plural-ism that necessitated a contractual union, a federal nation that was founded on liberties more than liberty. The American union followed well-established patterns among these Anglo-Americans: community is prior to government; the local and provincial is the parent to the larger and more cosmopolitan; Americans are unruly but self-ordering and so create governments through consent by way of contract, covenant and constitution; and group liberty is the irreducible condition upon which any constitution must rest.

From the earliest rumblings of what we now call the American Revolution until today, the most important fact about America as a people is that it is a plural people bound as much by mutual distrust as by a common and shared national culture. In a certain way—and by way of irony—the most enduring thread binding such radical difference to a shared government and national identity is liberty. The revolution was fought to protect liberties, the Constitution of 1787 was crafted in compromise to protect mutually exclusive liberties, the Bill of Rights of 1789 secured the union by protecting the lib-erty of the five regional cultures from the federal government, and today we will survive as a people only if the raucous spirit of liberty is greater in the American people than any collective sense of national purpose.

The American Revolution brought together the elites of very different cultures as part of a common cause against a singular threat to each region's liberty. From the late seventeenth century (essentially from the Glorious Revolution of 1688) to 1776 a new ruling class emerged in England, and this new class of elites posed an existential threat to the long-standing political freedom of the colonies and their long-established folkways. The new imperial ruling class in England created new institutions, such as the Bank of England and the East India Company, and adopted new ideas about sovereignty, law, and empire. They even cultivated new accents, reinforced through elite educational institutions like boarding schools, that demarked their new class from the rest of society. The cultural distance between Great Britain's power elite and the American colonial elites broadened with each generation.

With an imperial perspective, England's ruling class reorganized the empire in the years prior to the American revolution, consolidating and centralizing power. One illustrative example was the creation and expansion of the Admiralty courts, imposing a judicial system based on Roman civil law alien to one of the few objects of universal reverence in the American colonies, namely the common law, with its reliance on juries and the presumption of innocence. These changes not only overrode the different colonial elites but created more hierarchies, separating the system of justice from citizens. Colonial elites recognized the threat to their liberties and to their institutions, culture, and folkways. More than a "tax revolt," the American revolution was about the preservation of plural ways of living, plural cultures, and plural liberties against a powerful, centralized, distant, and homogenizing governing elite.

New Englanders, for example, fought for "public liberty," a rich concept rooted in their covenantal tradition. This collective form of liberty would be called "political liberty" or "township freedom" by Tocqueville, and it rests on the right or even obligation of a group of people to order themselves, as the Pilgrims did with their Mayflower Compact, the Puritans did with their Massachusetts Bay Charter—and, indeed, which all subsequent towns did in their charters. A community's obligation to order or organize itself in a godly fashion is also the freedom to create governments, and to create and enforce laws—on themselves. The freedom of the group—political freedom—to govern themselves often produced strange or unusual laws such as celebrations of local heroes or restrictions on activities found offensive only by the locals. Some local laws, such as strict bans on recreation of all kinds on the Sabbath, bred disobedience and even conflict. But something about the combination of political freedom and the eccentricity of each town's laws created a deep affection for the freedom to self-rule even when it came with severe individual restrictions.

The actions of parliament and the king in the decades leading to the American Revolution threatened to eliminate the dispersed political freedom of New Englanders, and when they prepared, in 1775, to organize resistance to the imperial power, they did so in typical New England fashion. Massachusetts called for a new representative assembly, with delegates sent from each town, tasked to organize resistance. In the process they both engendered and voiced the deep and widespread support of the citizens who had not only been consulted but who gave legislative warrant to rebellions. The New England revolution was most orderly, and it was an expression of popular sovereignty—one of America's fundamental principles. Other parts of the rebellion would express different principles and sentiments and none would be quite so orderly.

Massachusetts was the first to rebel to defend its kind of (public) liberty.[1] Virginia followed quickly, but for a very different kind of liberty or, rather, a range of liberties, suggesting the moral complexity of that culture. True to their colonial origins as supporters of King over Parliament, the most well-established part of Virginia, the Tidewater region, was committed to an aristocratic version of liberty that David Hackett Fischer labeled "hegemonic liberty." There is nothing "natural" about this kind of liberty, as it represented an inherited freedom (or right) to rule.

A birthright, hegemonic liberty implies rule over others but also involves two other kinds of liberty or rule: independence and governance over oneself. One of the most consistent observations of visitors to colonial Virginia was the independence of each plantation—the way each plantation served as a separate regime, close to sovereign over its territory. Such an emphasis on the independence of each plantation, along with the well-developed pattern of representatives from these plantations passing almost all laws that governed themselves, has been a persistent theme in American history—liberty as independence, which is to say freedom *from* interference.

Closely related to the importance of the independent self-rule of plantations was the belief in the necessary virtues of the gentleman. Focused on the liberty to govern one's own passions, this cultivation of the gentleman was tantamount to producing the kind of person capable of living in Aristotle's city—a person who has the virtue of ruling well, of being ruled well (by laws) and of deliberating well with fellow citizens. And as Aristotle assumed, to establish and maintain this kind of self-ruling republic, one had to organize the economy and society in such a way as to limit access to citizenship to those who had the means and the leisure to cultivate the requisite virtues. For the most established of the Virginia gentry, a republic was only possible when the many work and the few take on the obligations of ruling together.

The gentry of the Tidewater who inhabited this understanding of liberty not only altered a traditional concept of the laboring many and the ruling few with a racist system of slavery but also came more reluctantly to the cause of rebellion than other Virginians who hailed from the newer Piedmont region further west. The paradox of America's most ardent and eloquent defenders of liberty and natural rights coming from its slave region is deepened by what we might call the two Virginias.

While those of the Tidewater region eventually came to see the empire and its ruling class as a threat to their inherited privileges (i.e., liberties) and hence to their entire cultural and political self-understanding, the rebels of the Piedmont region—Thomas Jefferson, George Mason, George Washington, James Madison—quickly saw in British rule a threat to natural liberty. Natural Liberty is a term used by Fischer to describe the kind of freedom or liberty most associated with the Borderlanders, many of whom occupied land in Western Virginia. With one exception, the most influential rebel leaders of this region were not Borderlanders themselves, but their more refined and philosophically rooted concepts of liberty bear the influence of their more rustic neighbors.

Natural liberty or freedom rests on the belief that every animate creature has the right to life and to self-defense. Drawn from the chaotic and violent experiences of the borderlands of Great Britain and strengthened in the back-woods of America, this defense of liberty stressed freedom from government, from taxes, from meddlesome moralists (like Puritans and Quakers) even as it emphasized the right to "elbow room" for people—individuals, families, and clans—to live as close to nature as possible. As Fischer notes, these are not ideas of freedom drawn from John Locke or any other theorist so much as from the uncertain borderland life and the need to take care of one's own security, to protect one's own, and to defend the one thing that seems most sacred, the freedom to do as one pleases.

This is not a liberty that tolerates competing views—it is an exclusivist concept of liberty and tended to be enforced by strong, sometimes even violent, communal norms that encouraged both clannishness and sorting. In the case of Virginia, this point of view was best expressed by Patrick Henry, whose eloquence was always in the service of liberty from any and all dictates of distant power. Henry's penchant to label the king a tyrant as early as 1758 scandalized the Tidewater oligarchy while gaining him unstinting support among the sparsely populated and fiercely independent Virginians in the hinterlands. Henry would become not only one of the most ardent supporters of revolution ("Give me liberty or give me death") but also the state's first governor.

Few people typified the contradictions of Virginia as well as Henry. A vocal opponent of slavery, he remained, nonetheless, a slave owner. In this way he was similar to Thomas Jefferson, whose support of his own version of natural liberty ran through more philosophical channels yet rested his defense of liberty not simply on Lockean ideas, but on a strong belief that Americans (or at least Virginians) were reclaiming pre-Norman, Anglo-Saxon, liberties. And so American liberty was both an inheritance from the Anglo-Saxons and an expression of nature's laws. Slavery, in Jefferson's view, was a violation of both, and the fault of the king who had imposed this social malignancy on Americans.

Jefferson wanted the Declaration of Independence to not only spell out natural rights and the moral right of a people to self-rule, but also to place blame for the defining American sin on the king. While deleted from the final draft, Jefferson's argument on slavery is revealing:

> He has waged cruel war against human nature itself, violating its most sacred rights of life and liberty in the persons of a distant people who never offended him, captivating & carrying them into slavery in another hemisphere or to incur miserable death in their transportation thither. This piratical warfare, the opprobrium of infidel powers, is the warfare of the Christian King of Great Britain. Determined to keep open a market where Men should be bought & sold, he has prostituted his negative for suppressing every legislative attempt to prohibit or restrain this execrable commerce. And that this assemblage of horrors might want no fact of distinguished die, he is now exciting those very people to rise in arms among us, and to purchase that liberty of which he has deprived them, by murdering the people on whom he has obtruded them: thus paying off former crimes committed again the Liberties of one people, with crimes which he urges them to commit against the lives of another.[2]

Whatever else is going on in this passage, Jefferson finds in the king's actions a fundamental violation of the most basic norms of their Anglo-Saxon heritage as well as the principles of both natural law and Christianity. Here we have the most famous articulation of liberty in the context of natural rights written by a slaveholder. This was not just Jefferson's moral burden, it was Virginia's, though not South Carolina's, as we'll soon see. In Virginia the sacred liberty of some came bound with the enslavement of others. The defense of liberty was universal in both statement and belief even as those who believed this violated their own principles. However much Jefferson wants to blame others for his sin, his own principles reveal his complicity. Jefferson, Henry, and others were all too human, but their ideals of universal liberty cannot be undermined by the fact that Americans have engaged in evil any more than any of us undermine our truest beliefs by failing to live up to them. Only historical charlatans traffic in moral simplifications, failing to recognize the power of ideals and principles even as an American regime dared to affirm the highest moral principles as defining aspirations.

The ironies of Americans' plural understandings of freedom and liberty are many and the richness of these competing ideas count among our greatest inheritances. Not only do we find slavery and liberty bound together in some cases, but we also discover that the species of liberty that extends universally to all humans—the kind of freedom that would eventually become the rallying cry of the North in the Civil War—is not the product of Puritans or Yankees, but of slaveholders and frontiersmen. When New Englanders began their armed resistance to British rule, they were not fighting, as Colin Woodard noted perceptively, "for the universal rights of man, freedom of religion, or the liberties of their ruling class, but defense of the way they'd always lived their lives and regulated their affairs." They were defending local control, the primacy of THEIR churches and "their Anglo-Saxon birthright of freedom from tyranny."[3] By contrast to this provincial, judgmental kind of liberty,[4] the Virginian's offered an expansive libertarian idea that logically, necessarily, embraced some basic conception of equality of all humans and even, in some of its expressions, went so far as to suggest a fraternity of humans as would soon be promulgated by French revolutionaries.

Meanwhile, the complexity of American plural cultures and their concepts of freedom or liberty includes those who were less enthusiastic about revolution. For different reasons, Pennsylvania and South Carolina came to the rebellion reluctantly, and in both cases conflict with Borderlanders proved important. In the case of Pennsylvania strong pacifist influences along with a more positive relationship with Parliament, produced loyalist sympathies among most of the elite. Virginia's leaders pressured those in Delaware and Pennsylvania to join the rebellion, but it was Pennsylvania's domestic conflict between an eastern elite and the growing influence of Borderlanders that turned a loyalist region into a linchpin of the revolution. The far-flung communities of these Borderlanders up and down the Appalachian mountains all possessed a desire to be left alone, to be free from most outside constraints. In Pennsylvania this desire caused them to see the British as the greatest threat. Not only had the empire's elites restricted access to new lands farther west with the Proclamation of 1763, but the loyalists who largely controlled Pennsylvania government had all but excluded the Borderlanders from representation or any meaningful voice in politics. As a result, Pennsylvania Borderlanders considered both the Pennsylvania elite and the British government to be a common enemy to their independence.

The struggle for independence in the Carolinas took on a different character but for the same reasons. In both North and South Carolina, a long-hardening conflict (known as the Regulator movement) between coastal elites and backcountry folk had led to violence and a deep mistrust. While the slave lords of the Carolinas reluctantly joined the revolution out of growing fear that the British might inspire slave revolts, a good many of the Borderlanders fought on the side of the British in order to bring down the slave power elite. As in Pennsylvania, their fight was against oppressive elites and in defense of their "natural liberty." Some went into battle against the Carolina militias carrying banners that included the Scottish motto *"Nemo me impune lacessit"* ("no one provokes me with impunity") which is often rendered "Don't Tread on Me."

Loyalties and sides changed with circumstances, including British atrocities in the deep South, but the basic themes remain unchanged: this was a revolution 1) against an imperial elite who ruled without popular support 2) in defense of inherited liberties and self-rule, and 3) in anticipation of expanding the liberties that Americans most associated with the right to take care of themselves and their own without "outsiders" telling them how to live.

The regional, cultural sources of this revolution, then, were the primary forces shaping the kind of nation and national government that would emerge in the late eighteenth century. The states that united to form the nation did so in such a way as to protect their independence and to further their distinct ideas of liberty. Out of this emerged a plural nation. The nation was much like its Constitution: divided sovereignty between states and the federal government reflected a deeper struggle to find something common while preserving the rich cultural variety. Given that each culture loved liberty and that they each had reason to fear the power of a national government in the hands of any one culture, it is not surprising that the nation they crafted by choice and deliberation was dedicated to liberty as its defining national principle. And so out of many, one. The one, however, was, and remains, a plural one, a rich and complicated one, a beautiful and imperfect one.

NOTES

1. In his *Albion's Seed*, Fischer explores the complexity of this word "liberty" as used in New England—broadly understood as "ordered liberty." He identifies four distinct uses of liberty: collective liberty, individual liberties, soul liberty, and freedom from the tyranny of circumstances. The persistence of this constellation of concepts is quite fascinating, and, Fischer notes, stood behind the famous "four freedoms" promulgated by Franklin Roosevelt in 1941: freedom of speech and worship, freedom from want and fear. David Hackett Fischer, *Albion's Seed: Four British Folkways in America,* (New York: Oxford, 1996), 199–205, 410–14, 597–98.

2. Thomas Jefferson, *The Papers of Thomas Jefferson, Volume I: 1760–1776,* ed. Julian P. Boyd (Princeton: Princeton University Press, 1950), 426.

3. Woodard, *American Nations: A History of the Eleven Rival Regional Cultures in North America* (New York: Penguin, 2012), 128

4. The kind of liberty that would eventually supply American progressivism with its moral urgency.

Chapter 5

Conflict, Law, and Revolution

Colonizing is not for wimps. By 1624 between six thousand and ten thousand people had disembarked on American shores; fewer than 1,300 had survived. It got easier, or at least less fatal, as settlers figured out how to avoid being killed by predators, starvation, and local tribes. But vigor was essential to success in the New World. And success there was. From a population of five hundred in 1620, the European population of the continent grew to 2.75 million by 1780. Immigrants came in spurts, especially from Northern Ireland, Germany, and the Scottish borderlands, but more than three-quarters of the population growth came from births within the colonies.[1]

American colonists lived in constant tension between life and death, order and disorder, community and frontier. Conflicts between groups and between individuals and their tight-knit communities could be intense. Religious differences, personal rivalries, and commercial and land disputes all could spell trouble. Settlements, towns, and even colonies split off from one another. Individuals or small groups left their communities voluntarily or involuntarily, peaceably or through the sometimes-lethal means of being covered in tar and feathers and then carried out of town on a rail. Then again, townships often formed alliances and even federations to better protect themselves from the dangers of the new land. In short, at the heart of British colonization was conflict of many kinds, and the need to bring order to both control violence and protect liberties was a formative part of the American experience.

England was distant and mostly uncaring. Colonists had grown accustomed to this, indeed grown to appreciate it as a sign of their success and honor. Self-rule was, by the late eighteenth century, baked into the American character. Americans still pursued their interests in London, including by lobbying to have their colonial charters renewed, reinstated, or improved. They were constantly disappointed in this but fought to sustain and widen their powers of self-government, especially by resisting encroachments from royal governors and judges. British-appointed governors found themselves hemmed in by those who would be beneath notice in English public life but considered themselves "the better sort" in America. These merchants and landowners did their best to control judges by setting their salaries, resisted even low taxes, and left towns largely to their own devices. Colonists proclaimed their loyalty to the crown but treated their rulers mostly as nuisances. British trade restrictions and external taxes were avoided through rampant smuggling. British internal regulations were flouted or avoided, especially on the frontier. In America, even "the better sort" remained an unruly lot.

The culture that grew up during the century and a half of "salutary neglect" following settlement was dedicated to local self-government, a decidedly masculine code of honor and independence, and a pietism rooted in local congregations. Americans were unruly, but in a uniquely orderly way. Mobs could be a real danger to life, limb, and property. Duels continued to play an important role in American life all the way through the era of the gunfighter in the late nineteenth century. There were blood feuds among clans and race riots. But there also was a commitment to law—and to the deep and shared cultural norms that lay beneath law—that could transcend even deep, dangerous differences. One famous example makes the point. John Adams, chief mover behind Americans' Declaration of Independence, felt honor-bound to defend the British soldiers accused of murder for firing into a mob in what came to be known as the Boston Massacre. Adams's cousin, Sam Adams, worked hard to convict the soldiers in the court of public opinion. But the trial was conducted according to set rules and the defendants found not guilty of murder. Americans deferred to the law when it was their law, issuing from their culture and norms. In this crucial way, Americans obeyed themselves much as the Pilgrims bound themselves before God to the principles of God's law as understood by their tradition.

It may seem inevitable that such an unruly and litigious people would revolt against its colonial masters. An abundance of historians argue that the revolution was based in Americans' paranoia, their desire to oppress, and/or simple greed. In truth, the revolution was a surprise to participants and observers on both sides. Members of Parliament and royal officers could not believe that any reasonable colonist could find royal conduct worthy of revolt. Americans could not believe imperial governors could not recognize that they were violating their own constitution and driving away their loyal subjects. Even after fighting had begun, some Americans carried the British flag into battle against royal troops and British military leaders held out the possibility of pardons for the vast majority of the rebels if only they would lay down their arms.

Any dispassionate study of the causes of the American revolution would find truth and error on both sides. The British Parliament was acting consistent with its sovereign rights as they had come to understand them. The Americans wanted to be governed as they had been for well over a century;

when they declared "no taxation without representation" they weren't arguing for representation, they were arguing against taxes levied directly on goods and transactions. The British were in dire need of additional funds and saw no reason to spare troublesome Americans from being pushed into line as respectful colonials. Americans rarely stood in line for anything; they were "democratic" in that they recognized no absolute, unlimited power except God and would not surrender their developed liberties to a distant ruling class. Moreover, Americans' experience over generations had taught them that a combination of resistance, avoidance, and compromise would keep imperial forces at bay and so maintain their own self-government.

When American settlement began in the early seventeenth century, England was roiled by disputes over the king's claims to absolute power. For the rest of that century, civil war, restoration, and renewed revolution undermined claims of royal prerogative without establishing any full alternative. By the late eighteenth century Parliament had claimed that absolute power for itself but, whatever the case in England, the Americans were distant observers who saw no reason to accept that they could be ruled however Parliament saw fit, especially when that rule meant being taxed more, regulated more, and stripped of trial by jury and other rights they traced to English common law or, what was to them much the same thing, to long-standing practice in America.

During the eleven years between parliament's imposition of the Stamp Act and the colonies' Declaration of Independence, there had been a good deal of political debate over the nature of liberty and the constitution of the British Empire. Were Americans entitled to the rights of Englishmen, or did the common law stop at the water's edge in Britain? Were Americans fighting for English rights or abstract rights of man? Was American liberty natural? public? Hegemonic? Or some combination of all of these? Americans still argue over such questions, in part because what some see as our founding document—the Declaration of Independence—lends credence to almost every view imaginable as to why Americans rebelled.

Reasons for the confusion are many but are rooted in the nature of the document. The Declaration of Independence was a necessary legal act establishing Americans as a separate set of governments with their own duties and rights (including the "right" as a sovereign nation to continue receiving military assistance from the French); it also was a political statement intended to solidify support at home and abroad for the cause of independence. The Declaration constituted a kind of contract among new states—representatives of the thirteen colonies declared them to be "free and independent states" and, in reliance on Divine Providence, mutually pledged "to each other our Lives, our Fortunes, and our sacred Honor." Declaring that the King (and Parliament) had broken the contract binding them to the empire, it was a necessary prelude to establishment of independent governments, and the authors intended to reinforce a broad consensus among patriots (independence-minded Americans) regarding their reasons for rebelling. As such, the document looked to both soaring abstractions and specific, legalistic particulars to make its case. It included broad claims to natural rights and historically grounded claims of specific British violations of rights grounded in tradition and human nature. It looked to a tradition of political rhetoric going back to the English Declaration of Rights of 1688, through various petitions and declarations to Magna Carta, the Great Charter of 1215 by which English barons established the principle that even kings are subject to law. Some of the language would come to be called liberal because it emphasized personal liberty and natural rights; some would come to be labeled conservative on account of its insistence that it aimed only to preserve long-held rights against British usurpation. At the time, these differences were nearly invisible, and today's labels represent later categorical distinctions that isolate "ideas" and distort the historical complexity of the founding era.

Most commentators only discuss the first few phrases of the second paragraph of the Declaration, where the signers declare "We hold these truths to be self-evident." These "self-evident" truths set out abstract principles, especially that "all men are created equal" and that "they are endowed by their creator with certain inalienable rights." Recent decades have seen attacks on the drafters of this document for using the pronoun "men," and for failing to declare a long list of economic and other rights going far beyond "life, liberty, and the pursuit of happiness."[2]

The Declaration clearly asserts the natural law principle that we all are created in the image and likeness of God and so possessed of equal dignity and equal natural rights, which can be altered only through legitimate constitutional means within society. But the Declaration is far more than an abstract statement of natural rights. It begins with a recognition that one people is declaring independence from another people. The language is federal: "one people" (Americans) has found it necessary to "dissolve the political bands" connecting them with another people (the British). Americans first and foremost were members of families, churches, and townships. They also were Virginians or Massachusettsans; they were members of civil societies constituted by their states. In addition, but somewhat less foundationally, they were members of a broader people—they were Americans, even if the shared meaning of this label was unclear at the time. Finally, this people shared a more tenuous identity with other peoples within the British empire. That imperial identity was rather loose and derivative; in addition, it was legitimate only until "a long train of abuses and usurpations, pursuing invariably the same Object" made clear "a design to reduce them under absolute Despotism." This having been shown, it became Americans' right and duty "to throw off such Government, and to provide new Guards for their future security."

The bulk of the Declaration is made up of a long list of grievances (two dozen or more, depending on how one counts them) detailing acts aimed at "the establishment of an absolute Tyranny over these States." The list details instances of how the King (in practice generally Parliament)[3] had worked to eliminate American self-rule by keeping American legislatures from meeting, refusing to allow their acts to become law, and working to substitute decrees of royal governors for legislation. The King also had suspended long held rights, like that to be tried by a jury of one's peers, forced people to "quarter" troops in their homes, and taken away colonial charters. By these tyrannous acts he had "abdicated Government here, by declaring us out of his Protection and waging War against us." Faced with this reality, the Declaration's drafters called on "the Supreme Judge of the world" in declaring the American colonies to be "Free and Independent States."

The Declaration sought to call on and solidify a consensus among Americans regarding the nature of free government in America. It emphasized inherited rights to judicial fairness and, especially, rights of self-rule through colonial legislatures. There was room, of course, for British rule. But that rule was to be exercised, as it had been exercised, primarily as a check on overreaching from the colonies and as a set of imperial trade policies (policies which, to be sure, the colonists did their best to avoid). There was, in fact, no consensus on independence. No more than half the adult male population could be identified as active supporters of the Revolution. Loyalists, meanwhile, made up about 15 percent of this population. Remaining Americans were conflicted on the issue or merely sought to stay out of the fight. This meant, though, that the vast majority (about 85 percent) of Americans were no longer truly loyal to the British empire. And that, along with help from the French and a number of other factors, proved to be enough for independence.[4]

After independence, Americans were freed, not just from British rule, but also from the compromised political vision of colonists—valuing self-government but tied by oaths of loyalty to a higher sovereign across the sea. They had fought against long odds to secure independence. The stage had been set for a people to define its own political character within its communities, its states, and, potentially, something larger and more powerful.

NOTES

1. "Colonial and Pre-Federal Statistics," United States Census Bureau, 2004, accessed June 9, 2022, https://www2.census.gov/prod2/statcomp/documents/CT1970p2-13.pdf.

2. "The Declaration of Independence," in Bruce Frohnen, ed., *The American Republic: Primary Sources* (Indianapolis: Liberty Fund, 2002), 189–91.

3. Because the colonies were largely formed in agreements with the king and not from any charter issued by parliament, the colonials had to depend on the king to protect them from parliament if it acted on Americans without their consent, which is to say acted tyrannically. The failure of the king to protect citizens in the colonies from the unauthorized power of parliament was the technical cause for the Declaration of Independence to be directed at the king's actions or failures to act.

4. Thomas B. Allen, *Tories: Fighting for the King in America's First Civil War* (New York: Harper, 2011), xx.

Chapter 6

The Constitutional Conversation

The vast majority of patriots fought, not to make the world anew, but to prevent the British parliament from destroying their traditional rights and the institutions of self-government they had inherited and developed in the New World. The war itself was bloody and awful, of course. And those who defended the doctrine of "passive obedience" and unquestioning subservience to sovereign, imperial authority often found themselves victims of confiscation and/or mob attacks on their property, and sometimes their very persons. Tens of thousands fled and the remaining American Tories were politically and culturally marginalized; their political position became not merely unpopular but nonexistent. What remained was a general determination among Americans to devote themselves to practical pursuits: to continue settling new land, engaging in commerce, and governing themselves within their local communities.

Yet, even in the midst of determined localism, a certain radicalism attaches to every revolution. No one should be surprised that a war over whether a people had the right to govern itself would spawn radical thoughts and in America those thoughts took root in soil fertilized by religious enthusiasms and unruly characters. British-born, self-proclaimed "citizen of the world" Tom Paine wrote about the "common sense" of radical equality, and many Americans shared both his skepticism regarding inherited power and his faith in the common man. Pennsylvania enacted a rather radical first state constitution concentrating power in a single legislative body without check from an independent executive. When the French Revolution came, with its abstract declarations of the rights of man and its brutal elimination of aristocratic and spiritual hierarchies, it brought a bloody Reign of Terror in France, and a fair amount of support in America, for a time. Such support was encouraged by American dedication to consent and limited government, and by a lack of familiarity and a certain naivete concerning the complications of Europe's traditional hierarchies, their laws, and the angry tensions within their cultures.

Was there, then, a substantial, radical element in American political culture during the revolution, dedicated to a natural liberty divorced from tradition and common law? Events in succeeding decades weigh heavily against such a conclusion. Outside Pennsylvania, the new states adopted constitutions emphasizing the need to limit governmental power as well as the importance of local self-rule. Most influential was the Massachusetts Constitution of 1780. This frame of government, drafted by future President John Adams and still in effect, follows what had become the traditional American constitutional model. Its preamble declares that it is a compact for a political society, intended to protect its people's enjoyment of their natural rights and blessings. In listing such rights, the Massachusetts Constitution emphasizes procedural protections, for example barring unreasonable searches and seizures and guaranteeing free trials. It then provides a frame of government in which the legislative, executive, and judicial functions are kept separate through various checks and balances so that laws, not men, will rule.

Enjoying their now-unquestioned self-governance within their states, Americans resisted forming any meaningful "general" government. It took more than a decade of economic disorder and, in particular, the armed tax revolt in Massachusetts called "Shays' Rebellion" to convince George Washington, hero of the Revolution, to lend his crucial support for a convention to strengthen the confederacy. Concern to establish domestic tranquility, along with free movement of goods and a united front in dealing with foreign governments, eventually produced that convention, which spent as much time guarding against political overreaching as establishing federal powers.

The American Constitution does not make for exciting reading. There is no soaring, Jeffersonian rhetoric, only a straightforward preamble listing the general purposes of the "more perfect union" it establishes. Then again, our Constitution is not a statement of beliefs, let alone some radical ideological manifesto. The Declaration relied on general principles as well as specific charges of abuse to establish that colonists were right to secede from the British Empire. The Constitution's drafters had the more difficult task of setting up a general government to protect the freedoms and interests of Americans within their endangered states. As a frame of government, the Constitution is in essence a set of rules for making rules. It sets out powers and procedures for the various institutions—Congress, president, and Supreme Court—that will make, execute, and settle disputes under the laws. It binds the people to follow those rules and the laws they produce, but not to any specific set of substantive laws.

Americans may not find our Constitution exciting, but we are justifiably proud of it. We value it both for what it represents and for what it makes real. It represents our commitment to self-rule. It makes self-rule real, or at least possible, by limiting the power of federal and state governments, and separating that power among differing levels and branches. By its very existence it constitutes a government, making it possible to maintain order in the face of external threats and internal dissensions.

Crafted for an unruly people, recognizing every person's sinful nature, the Constitution guarantees peaceful, low-level conflict among and within branches of the federal government, as well as between the federal government and the states. Ambition will counteract ambition. The Constitution lays out process, not rhetoric, and focuses on mechanics, not philosophy. It sets forth rules establishing both institutional independence (tenure during "good behavior" for judges, for example) and inescapable occasions of potential conflict (the president's power to veto congressional legislation, for example), thereby protecting the separation and limitation of powers through checks and balances.

The Constitution reads like a contract or corporate charter. It gets into the gritty details of who is responsible for what (Congress is in charge of coining money) and who is forbidden from what (states can no longer levy taxes on goods from other states). It is an unapologetically practical and pragmatic document, embodying bargains on everything from general institutional arrangements to specific powers and limitations.

It is natural to think that the Constitution must be something more than a set of rules for making rules—that it must embody the hopes, dreams, and especially the ideals of the people. But this is to mistake the nature of a Constitution. Americans, no less than other peoples, have hopes, dreams, and ideals. But these deeply embedded, cultural aspects of life are not the stuff of constitutions. They are, rather, the stuff that constitutions depend upon and must protect.

Constitutions, like laws, are products of culture. They may influence or corrupt that culture, but they are not its source. Like mundane contracts for goods or land, social contracts can function only if there is sufficient shared understanding and friendship that the vast majority of the people the vast majority of the time will follow, uphold, and defend its terms without the need for enforcement mechanisms. No matter how attractive on paper, a constitution that does not fit the habits of a people will not serve that people, will not succeed as a social contract.

The sources of our Constitution lay in the people. The Framers called upon their understanding of history, law, and political theory in designing its mechanisms—especially the checks and balances that would maintain its separation of powers. The pluralism of American cultures produced conflict as well as an insistence on a federalism aimed at protecting local self-rule. In addition, however, they relied upon the people's underlying consensus about the virtues of limited government, the dangers of political power, and the duties of those in power to restrain themselves, to make the system work.

Republican government, as Publius argued in *The Federalist Papers*, relies more than any other on virtue in the people. But virtue cannot be created by the government; it is the product of families, churches, and other local associations in which people are taught what it means to be a good person, a good citizen, and a good public servant.

We already have seen the nature and grounds of the American consensus. Despite their many differences, Americans shared common experiences and characteristics sufficient to form a recognizable character—somewhat unruly, but deeply grounded in specific conceptions of faith, family, and freedom. Most important, here, was Americans' broad religious consensus. This may sound odd given how many religious denominations already existed in early America. But Americans' "dissension of dissent" was no indifference to religious truth, let alone rejection of religion's prominent role in public life. It was, instead, a recognition of America's e pluribus unum—out of many (predominantly protestant) sects there would be one broadly Christian people leading relatively virtuous lives while tolerating and even welcoming significant differences within their broader communities.

The word "religion" derives from a Latin root meaning "to bind." People worship in communities and those communities have common traditions and modes of practice in addition to core common beliefs. From early days, American colonies and townships had dominant religions, varying from one community to another. Some new states were more insistent than others on maintaining public support for particular religious institutions, but even states with "established" churches were extremely tolerant by eighteenth-century standards. For example, at the Revolution Massachusetts, Connecticut, and New Hampshire all implemented plans of religious assessment; they taxed all citizens for the support of religion. But no specific church was made the state favorite, let alone empowered to punish dissent. Rather, such laws provided support for various religious communities as each citizen directed his tax monies to the church of his choice. Several other states considered or even enacted similar provisions but did not implement them.

The general government was too distant and potentially powerful to be entrusted with any substantial role in local religious life and so the Constitution forbade it from interfering with state and local religious practices. Still, the general government's religious agnosticism was of a specific type—one respectful of an overwhelmingly Christian people and culture. Even the only vaguely religious Thomas Jefferson, often brought forth as a champion of "separation of church and state," as president regularly attended church services in the House of Representatives, continued support for Christianizing missions to the Indians, and made no attempt to interfere with state and local religious establishments. Meanwhile, Americans recognized

Christianity as a basis of their common law, upheld laws against blasphemy in the interest of public order, and continued to punish "moral" crimes like adultery and prostitution.

None of this is to say that Americans lived up to any ideal model of Christian life—either the rather passive model espoused so often today, or the dark vision of oppressive puritanism portrayed in twentieth- and twenty-first-century mythology. For example, the Bible was read in almost every American household, but churchgoing was far from universal. Dishonesty, hypocrisy, and violence were commonplace then, as now— though the label "sin" was more likely to be attached to such vices in recognition of their endemic and all-but-eternal nature. Accustomed to witnessing death from disease, beasts of the wild, and human violence, Americans were far more accepting of, and adept at engaging in, acts many today would deem brutal, and of subjecting others to their own will in ways more overt than today's bureaucratic structures.

Conflict between the lighter and darker sides of the American character were evident in the nation's greatest sin and tragedy, namely slavery. Several northern states already had extended increasing rights to those held in bondage and even moved toward gradual emancipation. In Virginia, Thomas Jefferson's draft of a state constitution in 1776 provided for its abolition. Southerners as well as Northerners decried the institution as an imposition from the British empire. Still, Southerners feared dominance from the more populous North and demanded excess representation for themselves by having the (obviously nonvoting) people they enslaved "count" in apportioning seats in Congress; they also demanded protection for the slave trade (it would last until 1808); otherwise, there would be no Constitution. Northerners, along with numerous antislavery Southerners, agreed to the resulting "Three-fifths Compromise" in part because of another underlying consensus—the mistaken view of most Americans that slavery would not last long in a free United States.

It is easy today to dismiss the Constitution's framers—and Americans of that era in general—as lacking in virtue because of their connection to what at the time was the global evil of slavery. But slavery's degradation of character would become far worse in coming decades. As to the founding generation, its members sought to live up to standards of virtue we would do well to remember and emulate. The prime example, here, is George Washington. In Washington we find the embodiment of American virtue, American consensus, and the tensions intrinsic to a society of unruly, self-governing people.

Every now and again pundits rediscover paintings and sculptures of George Washington, often dressed in a toga, looking for all the world like some Roman god. Derision, cynicism, and even outrage are expressed at such grandiosity, then the incident is forgotten. But Washington was no would-be god, nor were the lavish tributes to him considered out of place by most people in his time. Men of this era sought to emulate heroes, pursue recognition for their virtue, and seek rewards in both this life and the next through great actions.

Washington is well-known for patterning his life after the Roman hero Cincinnatus, the poor farmer who answered the call to lead his people in war, won that war, then returned to his plow. In battle Washington rode at the front, using his personal courage as a spur to bravery among his soldiers. As a public man he self-consciously sought the respect of others he thought virtuous by providing public service. In private he fought with his conscience, seeing to his finances to meet his obligations, including to free the people he held in slavery on his death.

The fame Washington sought promised self-respect on the grounds that one had won the respect of worthy others; it demanded restraint as much as action. He refused his officers when they entreated him to assume greater powers, made a show of resigning his military commission at the end of the Revolution, and refused to run for a third term as president at a time when many expected him to serve for life. Far from perfect, Washington could be a harsh master and commander, was criticized even in his own era for his studied formality, and made notable mistakes as a leader. For example, he approved formation of a national bank whose power to make loans rendered it constitutionally suspect. But he was no centralizer by contemporary standards. He signed the bank bill passed by Congress only after seeking the advice of both the nationalist Hamilton and the agrarian Jefferson. He upheld America's biblical culture by studiously attending a variety of religious services while president. And he bequeathed to his people an example of virtue that lasted many decades and in muted form to this day. He enshrined principles of civilian leadership of the military, limited terms for presidents, and the primacy of self-restraint as the key to personal virtue and good government.

Not long after Washington departed the scene, the partisan bickering he feared came to the fore in angry debates between his successor, the small-town farmer and Federalist, John Adams, and the new vice president, the large-scale plantation slave owner and Democratic-Republican Thomas Jefferson. The fight centered on constitutional construction (Jefferson sought to dismantle the banking system inaugurated under Washington) and, especially, America's attitude in the ongoing war between revolutionary France and Great Britain. The campaign was bitter, with Jefferson being labeled an atheist Jacobin and Adams receiving harsh criticism for signing the Alien and Sedition Acts which sought to forestall Jacobin immigration and punish malicious libel against the government and its members.

Americans held free if rancorous elections, and the result was respected. Adams went off to retirement and Jefferson assumed the presidency with promises of decentralization and constitutional restraint. The United States had survived its first change of administrations in a contested election. Then again, there was no real doubt that this would be the case, for Americans had been electing and replacing representatives for generations. The process, like the people, often was full of fire and fury. But it took place among people devoted to self-government under God in common with their fellows. We should not expect, however, that common conceptions of just what is involved in self-government would remain static, especially among a people famous (or infamous) for its variety of changing conceptions of God and the proper way to seek and worship Him.

Chapter 7

Cane Ridge and the New Protestant Consensus

In 1801, something powerful happened in the rural settlement of Cane Ridge, Kentucky. Reports told of a "revival meeting" that attracted huge crowds from hundreds of miles away. Thousands of people lay prone on the ground outside the little church building, struck down by some force and unable to move. Others began jerking manically, as though their bodies were controlled by an outside force. Some women jerked so violently that their long hair popped like a bullwhip. There was angelic singing in an unknown language and other signs of what Pentecostals would later call "glossolalia."

Spread across several acres, licensed preachers and lay exhorters stood on stumps or wagons, preaching or leading groups in prayer. Others danced or prayed, on their own or in groups. Huddles of people everywhere on the grounds produced a din that people claimed to hear miles away, like the sound of a great waterfall. Children as well as adults would rise from some spiritual exercise and begin exhorting others, often in language sophisticated and reflecting wisdom beyond their years and education.

More sober-minded observers wondered whether Cane Ridge was the work of the Spirit, or whether such anarchy suggested demonic influence. This was no "camp meeting"; that label would only emerge in 1802 as people began to create purposely what happened spontaneously at Cane Ridge. This was something wildly new but rooted in a sacramental gathering of the Presbyterian church, part of a long, established tradition going back over two hundred years to Scotland. In some ways it would mark the end of this long tradition (though versions continued long after) and the beginning of a new way of practicing religion that we now call evangelical.[1]

As with politics, so with religion. Revolution brought significant change to American institutions, beliefs, and practices. The reformed tradition, so essential in establishing American principles and habits of self-rule, constitutionalism, and virtue, remained at the heart of American culture. But it would evolve into a broader, looser collection of protestant forms more in keeping with the emerging American character. Central, here, was the evolution of an American species (and countless subspecies) of free-will Protestantism sometimes called Arminianism.

As a theological movement, Arminianism is rooted in Calvinist beliefs regarding predestination but insists that, as John Wesley, the founder of Methodism, put it, "God willeth all men to be saved, by speaking the truth in love."[2] Subspecies of Arminianism range from beliefs emphasizing the availability of God's grace along with each person's ability to refuse that grace, to Unitarianism, according to which all humans will, in the end, be saved. The common emphasis on individual free will, the possibility of achieving (rather than merely receiving) salvation, and the need to pursue a kind of personal and social perfection in this life all would deeply influence developments in American culture and character.

Historians have come to refer to Cane Ridge and its progeny as a "Second Great Awakening." The very term highlights the first Great Awakening as the critical development of Americans' Protestant culture. The first Great Awakening's outpouring of religious enthusiasm (and, as important, reasoned religious thought) represented a crucial return to traditional forms of piety in the increasingly prosperous American colonies of the early-to-mid-eighteenth century. Moreover, the fruitful conflicts within congregations and educational institutions between "Old" and "New Lights" that came out of the first Great Awakening became deeply embedded in American culture. Still, the earlier Calvinist revival remained deeply influenced by, and committed to, a hard-edged conviction regarding each individual person's predestination to salvation or damnation.

Too many observers insist on an absolute hostility between faith and reason, especially in the context of evangelicalism. The first Great Awakening was not, as many historians assert, an emotional movement hostile toward that other great eighteenth-century movement, the intellectual Enlightenment. In America, the Enlightenment was distinctly moderate, more indebted to English empiricism than to French rationalism. It shared with American pietism a belief in a natural order given by God, emphasizing both the limits on individual free will and the human capacity to order societies according to God's will. This predominantly English[3] pattern would be broadened and changed by new forms of piety, changed ethnic participation, and a new emphasis on individual free will.

The sacramental meeting at Cane Ridge was organized according to strict Presbyterian Calvinist ideas. But it would, in what was then the American West (Kentucky and Tennessee especially), deeply undermine people's faith in the key doctrine of the Reformed tradition, namely limited atonement. This was the belief that the sacrificial death of Jesus atoned for only some humans and not others. Cane Ridge proclaimed the availability of God's grace to all, and this transformation would be a harbinger for a theological and cultural shift nationwide.

In what would prove important, if not originally expected, the Cane Ridge meeting was both multiracial and multiethnic. In 1800 Presbyterians, whether in Scotland, Ireland, or America, were overwhelmingly of Scottish heritage. Religion and ethnicity had long been deeply connected for them and the rites and rituals of the church tended to offer opportunities for communal, ethnic solidarity as much as religious piety. In America the first major exception was racial inclusion where, particularly in North Carolina in the 1790s, Presbyterian churches often included a large percentage of black members. In fact, in America, the largest non-Scottish group in the church was African American. There were many black exhorters and participants. Methodist and Baptist preachers (who were non-Scots) spoke and participated. Countless people, without any license from any church, exhorted extemporaneously.

This ethnic and communal connection is crucial to understanding what happened at Cane Ridge and why it was the end of one tradition and the beginning of another. Because the Presbyterian Church has only two sacraments, conversion and communion, these rituals were freighted with great meaning and charged with deep emotions and passions. For two centuries Presbyterians had made periodic communion meetings the centerpiece of communal life. In this Lord's Supper, Christ was fully present (not the body and blood in the emblems, but his spirit was with the people taking the sacramental meal) giving to the event an often unstable sublimity and seriousness, mixing profound joy with anxiety, hope with fear. To participate in the communion, one had to be among the elect chosen by God. The process for this, among Presbyterians, was strenuous and well routinized. Diligent Bible-reading and careful catechesis were necessary for communicants to understand church doctrine and what to expect when God dispensed his grace.

The conversion toward which almost all members of the Presbyterian community aspired was traumatic, replicating in many ways the arduous journey of birth itself. Easy conversion, painless rebirth, was impossible. Atonement required the sacrificial death of Jesus. Who could contemplate that cost (required because of God's justice and human sinfulness) without enormous pain prior to the comfort felt in the full glow of received grace?

When church leaders organized a communion meeting, typically lasting several days, they would determine who was eligible to participate in the sacrament and the clergy would issue tokens for admission to the actual Lord's Supper. But hundreds or even thousands of others came who would not be admitted to the meal. The serious preparation (preaching and prayers) the day or two before the communion allowed those who had not yet felt God's grace to wait, in anticipation and hope, for their election to the saints. Emotions were high for both the elect and the sinner—both part of the same community—as one prepared for the most spiritually powerful event of the year and others waited in fear and anxiety for some clue as to their spiritual fate. The largest of these meetings were part carnival because they attracted people from surrounding communities who engaged in all manner of activities, from courting to business dealing. And yet, the stated purpose of the meeting was primarily for the saints to participate in a warm, affirming, and spiritually renewing sacrament with their brothers and sisters and, secondarily, to provide opportunities for the Holy Spirit to bring about conversion for others.

This was the model for Cane Ridge. But American conditions would break this mold and foster a new form of American Protestantism. That Protestantism was imbued with self-empowerment, high expectations for an improved or reformed society, and a broad egalitarianism that stressed opportunity more than outcome, and deemphasized ethnicity in favor of common humanity.

The most important Presbyterian-centered revivals prior to 1801 were in the Scotch-Irish sections of Western Pennsylvania, Virginia, and North Carolina. Almost all these meetings were connected to a series of "log cabin" colleges that trained ministers and became epicenters for revivalistic preaching. Most of the young ministers involved had ethnic ties back to Ireland and Scotland, but, importantly, a growing percentage were of English heritage.

By 1800 the region around Cane Ridge was enjoying stability and signs of prosperity. Most of the region's early ministers came from North Carolina or western Virginia, and so were culturally well connected to these new Kentuckians. One such preacher was James McGready. Like so many in his churches (he ministered to three congregations), his family hailed from Ulster, Ireland. He was doctrinally orthodox, classically trained in Latin and Greek, and he preferred a warm and emotional style of worship. When he arrived in 1796 he found widespread impiety, as one might expect among people who had not had regular access to the rituals and services of the church. McGready's work helped spark a cluster of revival meetings in the late 1790s that climaxed at Cane Ridge.

What happened in 1801, then, had much preparation and followed a pattern with roots in Scotland as well as America. The people who came to Cane Ridge knew what to expect, and yet got much more than they anticipated. The meeting was far larger, more ecumenical, and more diverse in terms of ethnicity and denomination (Methodist and Baptist preachers, present at previous meetings, were much more numerous and influential at Cane Ridge). A primary result was a reduction in the importance, or at least the centrality, of the Lord's Supper and the community-reaffirming nature of this sacrament. Cane Ridge would not be known for its purpose, but for its effects—the exciting, wild, often ecstatic religious ceremonies spread haphazardly across many acres and largely disconnected from the communion. In what seemed to many the work of the Holy Spirit, conversions of thousands took place, often by the exhortations of untrained and newly converted Christians or by barely literate Baptist preachers, among others.

But, while well-trained Presbyterian ministers no longer controlled events, the pattern of conversions at Cane Ridge refutes common historical narratives. If anything, conversions were more common among those of high social status and education, including the Governor of Kentucky, even as they included the most marginalized people in the area. Something new but not unprecedented was happening that extended through differences of class, race, and ethnicity creating demand for a kind of Christianity suited to this social and cultural environment.

In this shift, doctrinal differences would be the last (though in the end most important) thing to change. In the white-hot spirituality of Cane Ridge it was wondrous confusion—an almost "primordial" experience that defied inherited conceptualizations.[4] As this was happening, and in the months that followed, the most pressing question before the orthodox Presbyterian ministers was whether this outpouring of spiritual exercises, complete with claims to conversion, was the work of the Holy Spirit—or not. On this question rested much of American Christianity.

For orthodox Calvinists—those who adhered faithfully to the Westminster Confession at the center of Presbyterian doctrine—the Spirit works on those God chooses, taking the sinner on an arduous journey of rebirth that ends in the overwhelming beauty and calm of God's gracious election. For most Reformed churches, culture, experience, and careful catechization developed predictable patterns in this process, helping to assess the authenticity of the conversion. But in all cases the Spirit worked on the sinner; the sinner could not choose conversion.

The sinner has no say in this process, according to orthodox Calvinists, because he has a corrupt will. Though physically free, the person is enslaved by his depraved will and so lacks the moral freedom to choose God over self. It is the work of the spirit to liberate him from his corrupt will and, in the process, reveal the all-compelling beauty of God—who will become the new object of his love. Without such action by the spirit, the person is condemned, in this life and the next, by his own depravity. The harshness of this teaching, which has the virtue of reaffirming the sovereignty of God but also, to some humans, exposes God's capriciousness and introduces a logical human fatalism, was the subject of enormous complexity in teaching and practice. Most Presbyterians affirmed the doctrine of limited atonement and predestination with all manner of qualifications.

Many saw the spectacular display of spirituality at Cane Ridge as proof that God had used this event to do amazing work in reviving and regenerating

His church. This was how they had understood previous revivals. But there was more at work here. The ethnic and religious pluralism of the west would introduce a new kind of competition for members and at Cane Ridge the "free will" doctrine of Methodists and even some Baptists proved to be an advantage. If Jesus died as a sacrifice for all humans, then the question of a person's salvation was in the hands of each person, not God's. Preaching and exhorting, singing and praying—these were means of reaching the sinner's heart and persuading him to make the choice, to accept God's offer of salvation made possible by God's astonishing blood sacrifice. The Holy Spirit, in complicated ways, would be part of this process but as a gift to the person who has chosen to convert rather than as the instrument of God's choosing to bring the elect to grace.

Emphasizing individual human choice, Arminianism was attractive to a people who yearned to know the spiritual blessings of God's love and believed in each person's power over his own fate. Its influence over American Christianity grew exponentially over the next thirty years. The Presbyterian church in the area would undergo severe splintering as successful ministers replicating the methods of Cane Ridge were accused of Arminianism and church members tried to come to grips with the doctrines of their church. Two of the most important ministers involved would eventually join the Shaker movement, America's first Pentecostal church. Barton Stone, who was the minister at Cane Ridge at the time of revival, got caught up in investigations about his fidelity to the Westminster Confession. Stone eventually broke with the Presbyterian church and "Stonites" preached a rather radical view of atonement and even of the Godhead, rejecting traditional views of the trinity. In due course, most of the churches associated with Stone joined with congregations associated with another former Presbyterian minister, Alexander Campbell, to form what we now call the Restoration Movement.

Ethnic, doctrinal, and communal ties fractured. There was no going back. And the extraordinary variety found in American Christianity in the Second Great Awakening suggested nothing so much as a great emphasis on human agency and the power of faithful Christians, working voluntarily in churches they created, to change (save) individuals, and also their society.

Beginning in 1802, churches began holding "camp meetings" intended to convert as many sinners as possible. These new style meetings no longer centered on ethnic ties or sacraments. Organizers and ministers from many different denominations innovated and borrowed techniques as they learned how best to create an atmosphere conducive to conversion. Most preachers employed a very emotional and usually extemporaneous style of sermon. New hymns focused on the joy of salvation and God's all-powerful love prepared people to see that they only needed to accept God's invitation—open equally to all humans—for all His promised blessings to become theirs. Later innovations, like the "anxious bench," focused on people whose anxiety about their own sin, fear of damnation, and/or doubt about whether God could truly love them, encouraged these souls, in front of hundreds or thousands of Christian supporters, to step out of darkness and into the light. Many variations of these meetings emerged. There were denominational and regional differences, but one overwhelming goal: to persuade people that their salvation was ultimately their own choice and that God awaited them with unimaginable gifts, including eternal salvation, once they made that choice.

What came to be called "that old-time religion" was actually quite new. And the innovations of revivalistic, evangelical Arminianism would have significant effects on culture and society.

First, revivals almost always brought with them increased focus on social reform. Beginning with the early Presbyterian revivals in Kentucky, they created anti-slavery petitions to be sent to the state government. Many other reform crusades would emerge both locally and then, with increased cooperation and organization, become regional or national. Evangelical Christians sought to control the bad effects of alcohol through temperance movements and worked to outlaw many vices that plagued their communities. They were quite willing to use governments (usually local and state governments) in their reform crusades.

Second, because this type of Christianity concentrated so much on the individual person in his journey toward salvation, it reinforced and exaggerated the tendency in American life toward voluntary or chosen communities over those inherited or connected to ethnicity or other non-chosen attachments. Churches operated in a market for members and while the choices people made to create a church by contract or to join existing congregations were typically earnest and led to deep involvement in the work of that congregation, they depended on the willingness of the individual person to remain part of that group. By the 1820s and 1830s, this feature of American religion produced a fluidity, an openness to experimentation, a "ferment"[5] of churches and religious groups, that has few, if any, parallels in history.

Third, experimentation came to characterize American Christianity (and groups that were not Christian) and reinforced several conflicting American character traits. For example, some groups rejected ferment and fluidity by creating intense communities based on ethnicity and doctrine and found, in the great expanse of the American land, freedom to live alternative lives. Groups like the Hutterites, Mennonites, and Amish, among others, thrived. Other groups experimented with communal living and alternative lifestyles—from Shakers to the Oneida community, among hundreds of other groups. This community building, based on shared ideas and hopes, had been central to American life since the Pilgrims, and like so many of these more extreme versions, was often short-lived.

Other new religious communities became large and lasting, sometimes with ideas that were quite threatening to Christians around them. The most famous and enduring were the Mormons (The Church of Jesus Christ of Latter-day Saints) whose teachings included new revelations from God to their founder, Joseph Smith, and hence a Christian heresy (a teaching shared by almost all Christians in the era) called Antinomianism. This claim to moral freedom from obedience to established law (and several Mormon practices flowing therefrom) made them pariahs and sent them on a journey west that, after much violence, forced them to what would become the Utah territory. Another group, the Millerites, believed in the imminent second coming of Jesus, expected in 1843. The believers sold all their possessions and waited in anticipation for the wondrous event. Unlike many other groups that dispersed after a failed prophecy, the Millerites survived and even thrived as Seventh-day Adventists. All of these groups reveal an American genius for creating community, for building associations from new ideas as much as from shared needs. Individualism in America—as evidenced by the most individualistic form of Christianity—was always connected to community building.

Fourth, Evangelical Christianity in America focused on social equality. This focus could take extreme or categorical forms in groups like the Shakers. It also manifested in more generalized beliefs about the nature of popular sovereignty in politics (the importance of having the "people's voice" be heard) and various reform movements that attempted to mitigate or eliminate certain forms of inequality (slavery being only the most obvious) or worked on behalf of marginalized members of society, such as criminals and the insane.

Fifth, one of the most enduring effects of American-style Arminianism was a focus on the power of each person, not only to work toward his salvation by accepting Jesus, but also to craft the best possible self. Central to this species of individualism was the social equality that declared every person's power to become "self-made"—a person who possesses the highest qualities appropriate to human life and nature. The task of self-cultivation, long emphasized among aristocrats who devoted years to education and self-discipline to produce the virtues associated with honor, was now something possible and, indeed, emphasized, as a moral obligation of all people. Every man should be a gentleman and every woman a lady, even if the "look" of these types differed dramatically and often regionally.

As we will see in later chapters, the centerpiece of American character— the conviction that each person, no matter where he falls on the social scale, has the ability and obligation to devote himself to self-improvement—was tethered to a normative vision of the human. To be a self-made person in 1840 was not to be at liberty to create a new identity based on one's whim or desire, but to understand, internalize, and then exhibit the virtues appropriate to a good and noble or honorable life. These virtues were classical in some ways (reason must be the master of passion) but deeply influenced by Christian teachings on virtue and by certain threads of America's moderate Enlightenment.

There was a danger of perfectionism in Arminianism. Latent from the beginning, dominant in peripheral movements like the transcendentalism of later decades, and at the core of secularized religions of the late twentieth century. This extension of dreams of self-mastery, always present in the hearts of all persons, was made possible by the individualism of Evangelicalism. This is not to say, however, that Evangelical Christianity, that most American of religious movements, was doomed to become the prideful utopianism of later ages. Its most important religious tenet, that each person has the capacity to achieve nobility and salvation, is shared by that supposedly most passive, retrograde of religions: Catholicism. Often caricatured as a calculus of good works and sin, the Catholic understanding of each person's struggle for salvation emphasizes the need to orient the soul through faith in action. A properly formed conscience shapes right actions of virtue and atonement, helping shape a soul capable of accepting God's grace. Once historically grounded animus and differences in style and vocabulary are put aside, this vision shares much in common, at the practical level certainly, with Evangelical Christianity.

In the welter of religious movements stemming from the Second Great Awakening there was room for community as well as individual, humility as well as pride, and determination to conform oneself to a higher order as well as utopian dreams. Conflicts among these motivations added to the variety, conflict, and order of American life. They also made possible, in the midst of hatred, self-love, and other sins endemic to human nature, maintenance of a free society, in which the individual's drive to dominate was held in check by the covenants, contracts, and folkways handed down among an unruly, settler people.

NOTES

1. "Evangelical" refers to a Christian who stresses a crisis conversion experience followed by a personal relationship with Jesus and a warm, emotional style of worship less focused on doctrines and more on moral conduct.

2. John Wesley, *Works*, vol. XIV (London: Wesleyan Conference, 1872), 279.

3. This is not to say the Scots had not already had significant influence on American intellectual life. Presbyterianism already had played a significant role in America, as had the Scottish Common Sense school, with its emphasis on conscience as the proper guide to action.

4. The historical literature on Cane Ridge is very uneven and much of it written in support of denominational histories. The best work for placing this event in the context of larger historical, doctrinal, and cultural trends is Paul Conkin's *Cane Ridge, America's Pentecost* (Madison: University of Wisconsin Press, 1990) and Conkin's book is the most important historical resource for this chapter.

5. One of the great classics of American historiography, and a book that is endlessly fascinating and delightful in its depiction of this "ferment" of religious expression is Alice Felt Tyler's *Freedom's Ferment: Phases of American Social History to 1860* (Tokyo: Case, 2007) originally published in 1944.

Chapter 8

"The Democracy" and Its Limits

George Washington died just before the nineteenth century began, soon before John Adams lost the presidency to Thomas Jefferson, and in the midst of America's struggles to gain its footing as a new nation in a dangerous world. Many Americans lamented that their country had lost its greatest defender and exemplar of public virtue. Others looked forward to a more democratic and egalitarian future, in which great men would play much less of a role.

It was inevitable that succeeding leaders would descend from Washington's heights, willingly or not, even within the founding generation. Adams was brilliant and hardworking but lacked political temperament. Jefferson was urbane and well-spoken but unwilling to confront French or British aggression and had difficulty putting his strict construction of the Constitution into practice. James Madison slipped into a near-catastrophic war with Britain that brought the burning of Washington, New Englanders' threats to secede from the United States, and no victory.

Such setbacks did not define the American story. Politics was peripheral to American self-identity. This may sound odd, given Americans' pride in themselves as a free people, but the essence of self-government is less political than social and cultural. In their own minds what made Americans special was their ability to lead decent lives on their own, with "on their own" meaning "alone" only rarely, within their natural communities most commonly, and, perhaps most importantly, predominantly within their townships.

Politics was important, of course, as was government administration. Even in the early colonies there were tasks, from road building to waging war, that had to be taken care of by people to some degree separated from family, church, and voluntary associations. Not even the New England town meeting could take care of all the public's business without imposing some duties on persons chosen, for however brief a period, to carry out the will of the people. And even a limited federal government made the distribution of powers and responsibilities more complicated. No constitution could fully spell out and nail down all potential forms and spheres of action. Disagreements or "turf wars" were inevitable over precisely who should take exactly what action to head off dangers or identify and improve public goods.

Such disagreements cannot be explained predominantly in ideological terms because no single vision could structure a free society, let alone one as complex and diverse as the United States. For example, for many decades historians and others claimed that Americans in the early republic were—for good or ill—decidedly hostile to any kind of government interference with business and commercial activities and utterly opposed to any government provision of any kind of public goods or services. More recent observers have sought to conjure in early America an emerging social democratic state limited only by the primitive conditions of the time and place.

What both sides forget is Americans' ability and determination to forge practical solutions to everyday problems. Laws and customs regulating economic activity, prohibiting nuisances (for example forbidding people from keeping large stores of gunpowder in populated areas), policing the public square, and providing for the needy were common in American townships. As throughout the United States, the mechanisms of self-government were restricted, but at the local level aimed at serving a public good seen in expansive, communitarian terms, rooted in a determination among townspeople to take care of their own.[1]

Part of the political conversation central to American life was an instinctive attachment to a complicated notion: what Alexis de Tocqueville dubbed "administrative decentralization." The complex machinery of national government constituted a set of rules for distributing and limiting powers but, more fundamentally, protecting spiritual and organic relationships in the localities. The business of government ("administration") was significant at the local level but much less so at the state and national levels. Consequently, the powers of self-government exercised in the townships—and in families, churches, and voluntary associations—was great. In brief, the real action and the substance of life were neither national nor specifically political, but local.

Tocqueville spends the bulk of his magisterial *Democracy in America* analyzing the American township. He explains how townships come to be (naturally), how they function (predominantly through a web of norms or "habits of the heart"), and how (by teaching the art of association) they protect liberty from the excesses of equality and the drive for conformity. We do not intend to repeat Tocqueville's analysis but think it important to follow his lead in emphasizing that cultural and social life, and not political activity, were central to American character.

It is fortunate for America that politics was not the driving force of American life in this era, for it was a deeply troubled and destructive time, politically. The "antebellum" or pre–Civil War era was one of consistent political failure at the national level, culminating in the Civil War. But to tell this story on its own, or even to emphasize it within a discussion of the United States during this time, is to mischaracterize American life and character. National politics was seen and valued primarily through the prism of local, practical concerns.

The most dangerous political innovation of this era was the political party. Washington was perhaps the most vocal of the Framers in expressing the common opinion that political parties are highly dangerous to republican government. In his Farewell Address, Washington urged the people to reject "the spirit of party," by which he meant the kind of partiality or dual loyalty that would cause public figures to lose sight of the common good in pursuing their own narrow, organized interests. Different opinions regarding the public good were inevitable, especially in a compound republic, in which each township had its own set of public goods to defend and balance with the goods of other localities as well as the more general, limited goods of state and nation. It was the job of the federal government to balance and meld these goods, most often by preventing rather than taking action at the federal level. This would be possible, as Publius explained in *The Federalist Papers*, because particular factions would not be able to control a majority in Congress; there always would be enough members with no particular interest in the conflict at issue, to allow the public good to prevail.

The spirit of party would change all this by bringing narrow interests together into grand coalitions—to make deals inconsistent with the overarching social contract. The partial visions of the public good fostered by party loyalty would lead to a loss of public virtue as concentration on party victory obscured the full, genuine public good. Politicians, seeking to win elections for their parties, would lose sight of their own proper limitations, overpromise the electorate, and otherwise subordinate the common good, and especially the Constitution, to the particular goods of their party. This critique was no naive (or proto-tyrannical) demand that everyone share a common vision of what makes for a good life but, rather, a concern that natural differences of opinion and interest regarding federal policies should not be formalized into party programs and party machinery.

The Adams/Jefferson split produced a nascent party structure before Washington had even left office. Its effects were limited, however, by the fact that, with their electoral victory, the Jeffersonian "Democratic-Republicans" were forced to come down from their leader's more ideological statements and govern in a fashion not overly hostile to the American consensus. Jefferson concentrated on restricting federal actions and powers, in essence maintaining the primacy of state and local customs and institutions. Later on, however, the spirit of party would be reborn in a more virulent form, producing many of the evils feared by the Framers.

After Washington, the first president termed "great" by American historians was Andrew Jackson. Jackson clearly was a sign and source of change
in the body politic. Often contrasted with his rival, John Quincy Adams,
Jackson until relatively recently was portrayed as the great democratizer. An
orphaned son of poverty, Jackson beat the high-brow son of John Adams in
America's first relatively mass-scale election, held in 1828. He portrayed
himself, not as a mere servant of the public, but as champion and defender
of "The Democracy," sent to save the forgotten common man from corrupt
political elites and anyone who stood in the way of westward expansion. He
would produce the first effective party system in the United States, and with
it the makings of constitutional decline.

As with most historical figures, Jackson in recent years has been subjected
to rather vicious attacks for not being a contemporary leftist. In Jackson's
case, however, there is a real basis for reevaluation. He was not only a slaveholding planter, but one who sought to hide the fact that he actively engaged
in the business of buying and selling slaves. He was a dishonest and brutal
broker and breaker of deals with the Indians. He brought corruption and
personal invective to national politics on a scale previously unheard of in
America. At the same time, it is important to note that his "spoils system" was
an important factor in establishing and maintaining self-government by the
American people. Eliminating most permanent federal offices, Jackson saw
to it that public officials served at the will of the people, rather than at the will
of any separate elite with its own interests separate from that of Americans as
a whole. Party differences and corruption undermined the practice of public
service but pushed off for many decades establishment of a "neutral" set of
elites who would rule in their own interests, pursuing their own self-interested
and self-regarding notions of the public good.

Jackson was extremely successful as a politician, winning the presidency
in two landslide elections and forging a party that dominated American
politics for decades. But he had many adversaries. Most prominent, over
time, was Henry Clay, a Kentucky planter whose Whig Party promoted an
"American system" aimed at expanding national power to manage the money
supply, build roads, and otherwise pave the way for national development. In
a repeat of the Jefferson/Hamilton conflict, Jackson defeated such proposals
in the name of limited government and the people's right to be left alone; he
thus forced infrastructure projects back into the states and localities, where
there was no doubt of their constitutionality.

A more colorful and culturally relevant Jackson adversary was Davy
Crockett. Crockett shared Jackson's lack of formal education but combined
it with a genuine concern for the well-being of poor farmers. Crockett came
to Congress as a Jackson ally, determined to help the common man. But
Crockett broke with Jackson when the president successfully opposed his

attempts to gain relief for poor settlers facing a highly complicated system of land grants that favored speculators. The break became complete when Crockett opposed Jackson's forced removal of peaceful, settled Indians from their lands east of the Mississippi—removal made in pursuit of land and gold, and producing the murderous Trail of Tears. Crockett, who called Andrew Jackson "a greater tyrant than Cromwell, Caesar, or Bonaparte," lit out for Texas, where he died defending the Alamo.

Crockett was a Whig, like Clay, devoted to a national money supply and internal improvements. But his feud with Jackson was as much a matter of character as policy. Crockett sought to use the national government for national ends. Whatever one thinks of such Whig policies, he was most concerned with issues beyond his own power and pride. The Democratic Party, like the Whigs, including many men of public spirit, sought to promote limited government and the flourishing of American life. Whigs united behind a vision of increased federal spending on public works and a more stable, national system to control the currency. Jackson's Democratic Party ended up opposing such increases in federal power, but also supporting a system of "pet banks" to handle government money and a spoils system that encouraged corrupt office-seeking and cronyism along with the corrupt padding of public payrolls. Most ominous, Jackson's democracy was committed, not merely to Western expansion but also to an aggressive program of conquest intended to buttress the fortunes of the slave power.

Jackson and Crockett represent two sides of the political fallout from cultural change in America. The falling away of British rule and influence, along with the elimination of American Tories as a political force, undermined the remnants of class structures still existing in early America. Jackson's Democracy was an extreme manifestation of a long-standing, overall trend toward greater political equality—a trend Crockett's brand of Whig politics also embraced. As Tocqueville noted, increasing democracy—the march of equality—was more or less inevitable in some form. The question was how the American people would respond to it and incorporate it into their communities.

A pattern was already emerging for the integration of democratic norms into public life. That pattern would be given shape and motive force, as so often in America, by a set of religious beliefs and practices that had their roots in the Old World but were made particularly American by the circumstances of a new land and the character of a people devoted to both individual will and communal engagement, and both the search for salvation and the determination to make the most of opportunities in this world. Cane Ridge had helped form these patterns. Succeeding developments would reshape them.

NOTES

1. Perhaps the most important work on this topic is William Novak, *The People's Welfare* (University of North Carolina, 1996).

Chapter 9

Changing Circumstances, Abiding Character

One of our central concerns in this book is understanding how American character has remained consistent over four centuries even as America, like the world, has changed so dramatically. In later chapters we will confront our political and academic class' insistence that the Civil War and its aftermath fundamentally changed the nature of our republic and, from that, our people. But, before examining the reasons why this common view is dangerously mistaken, we first must lay out the pattern by which the American tradition has sustained itself and its people. Only then can we understand the abiding core of American character through the cataclysm of Civil War, the seeming revolution of Reconstruction and consolidation, and the economic dislocations and transformations of mass-scale industrialization.

When Tocqueville visited America, he saw its essence in the township. These small communities (tiny villages by today's standards) governed themselves in all things public and private. Self-government in the township was essential to sustain both free institutions and free characters. As Tocqueville put it, "Town meetings are to liberty what primary schools are to science; they bring it within the people's reach, they teach men how to use and how to enjoy it. A nation may establish a free government, but without municipal institutions it cannot have the spirit of liberty."[1]

Americans' spirit of liberty was not mere individualism; it was lived in and for the community, rather than for individual self-satisfaction. Again, Tocqueville: "It was never assumed in the United States that the citizen of a free country has a right to do whatever he pleases; on the contrary, more social obligations were there imposed upon him than anywhere else."[2] American communities were intrusive; they required much of their citizens and there was none of today's obsession with individual privacy. Until well into the twentieth century, for example, people in western and midwestern towns often did not put drapes on their front windows, seeing no reason to

81

hide their parlors from the neighbors. Public spaces from the church to the lobby of the local hotel (generally the town's grandest building) were places of easy familiarity but strict, common rules demanding good behavior.

Local citizens expressed their independence through public debate and, more important, through control of their own households. They were full human beings, confident in their own powers, insistent upon their own rights, and determined to be heard in the public square. The creeping danger to their community, Tocqueville noted, was that citizens would retreat from the rough-and-tumble of public life into individualism, by which he meant the mere enjoyment of home and hearth while abdicating the responsibilities of self-government.

Withdrawal from social life meant withdrawal from one's full self, to the impoverishment of both one's soul and one's community. Despite appearances, American self-government was not spontaneous; it was, rather, the outgrowth of social habits developed over time. New England Puritans came to the New World with such habits, having developed them in their covenantal, church communities, as did Scots Presbyterians raised in their tight, congregational communities. Other immigrants developed them, some more easily than others, by interacting with longer-term Americans and by confronting circumstances on the frontier. Isolation and danger from wild animals and potential armed conflict required cooperation on a fairly constant basis. And, as Tocqueville observed, people naturally want such cooperation to be relatively pleasant and so develop habits of cooperation to smooth the way. The result was a plethora of voluntary associations concerning everything from grain storage to religious salvation to singing. The result also was a particular kind of person, who saw himself as independent and self-governing in significant measure because he was a full member of his communities.

Washington's public embodiment of the Cincinnatus myth was no accident. Cincinnatus was merely the highest form of a widespread ideal type brought over from England with the earliest settlers, namely, the yeoman farmer. This ideal of the independent head of household and full participant in public life matured in America to the more democratic ideal of the freeholder. Heads of households sought, above all, financial independence. To own one's own land "free and clear" and run one's own household is an ideal with the deepest roots in our civilization. It came to fruition in the township where independence and commercial ambition combined with the demands of life on the frontier and a temperate honor-seeking through public service. The habits of public participation Tocqueville noted built the local roads, captured criminals, and rebuilt barns and entire towns in the wake of disaster.

There were tensions in this life. Tocqueville feared both individualism and the conformity born of the democratic pressure to go along with the public consensus. Yet these forces contended, within an unruly people, to maintain the character of both the person and the township. In particular, Americans were expert at forging "deals," whether through formal documents or informal bargaining, to foster cooperation and minimize disputes by settling specific terms and procedures for themselves. In addition, the relative ease of migration, aided by a sometimes-grasping and even brutal land-lust, served as a safety valve of sorts—a true, serviceable right to exit—to deal with internal dissensions. A commonsense acceptance of the limitations of settler life also helped maintain a public liberality that fostered cooperation; the town church, for example, often was built before a preacher could be found, and permanent ministers often could not be found for long stretches of time, and so residents generally were happy to hear from ministers of a variety of (protestant) denominations. Even the seemingly omnipresent local colleges, usually founded by a particular denomination, were decidedly open to both staff and students professing a variety of faiths. Finally, the spirit of voluntarism and long-standing administrative decentralization kept state interference in check and provided scope for personal ambitions.

It is easy to dismiss the township as an historical curiosity of no relevance today. But its real heart was the notion of self-as-freeholder. And this vision has proven vigorous in the face of sustained assault from ideologues and circumstances. Mass migration and the rise of large-scale, national behemoths of power, including railroads, banks, and the federal government, failed to stamp it out. Instead, the late nineteenth century would see essentially a repeat of the protestations of Crockett's time; freeholders would consider even radical political action, but only when and to the extent it aimed at restoring and protecting their freeholds. Even urban workers in America showed their continued attachment to this self-conception by rejecting socialist activism in favor of labor contracts providing "living wages" aimed at mass ownership of private, single-family homes. As we will see, only a specific form of home-grown radicalism could undermine the essential, overlooked grounds of this vision in religion and traditional family life. Even then, this vision remained deeply rooted in the American character, sustaining norms holding off for many decades the final triumph of progressivism.

What, then, were the massive changes of the early nineteenth century, and how did Americans face them? We have mentioned the initial democratization of society in the wake of the Revolution: apprentices moved out of their masters' homes; outside the South even minor gentry increasingly surrendered signs of their social superiority; and the vote was extended to almost every white male. But these genuine changes, erasing the last vestiges of colonial deference, merely strengthened the banks channeling the mainstream of American cultural life. More far-reaching were changes to the economic realities within which Americans lived, the shape of America's public philosophy, and the demographic makeup of America itself.

Early industrialization brought factories to American towns and cities well before the Civil War, along with associated problems of urban life. The effects, for example on the family economy (in which husbands, wives, and children often worked together to produce limited quantities of manufactured goods for sale) were significant. But changes to people's characters were limited by a number of factors: first, factories first grew up in rural areas in America, that is, without the extreme concentration of population and loss of distinctive local life so often experienced in crowded cities; second, widespread fear of moral degeneracy resulted in equally widespread measures to uphold traditional values within factory life; for example, many factories insisted on hiring only all-female work forces, with each employee living in a chaperoned dormitory until her eventual exit, generally through marriage.

Far more damaging, if unplanned, was the renewed profitability of slavery. In 1808, as soon as allowed by the Constitution, Americans closed themselves off from the international trade in slaves. A disastrous side effect of this obvious moral advance was a massive increase in the value of slaves already in the United States. At the same time, new manufacturing techniques (usually summed up in a single invention, the cotton gin) rendered slavery, long an economic loser as well as a moral stain, suddenly hugely profitable. Slave owners became far more attached to the "peculiar" institution as new profits added greatly to their power and influence. All too many internalized a false vision of reality that justified such temporary economic advantages through the false science of racism and a warped conception of aristocracy, both at odds with the broad currents of American common law and Christian morals.

Americans' concern with moral development also changed. We always had been reformers, sometimes even enthusiasts of utopian experiments, though unusually open to abandoning such experiments when they proved damaging to people's concrete lives. New reformers sought to improve prison conditions, secure better treatment of debtors and the insane, and address the problem of rampant alcoholism. Here too, the results often were not salutary. For example, the mania for silent, solitary confinement of prisoners drove many literally out of their minds. But the drive for improvement remained deeply embedded in the American character.

Americans always had been consumed with the idea that they should improve, not just their material well-being, but their characters and, of course, the state of their souls. One significant trend is best represented in the figure of Presbyterian minister Charles Finney. Finney's was a brand of spiritual perfectionism reminiscent of the most utopian of the Puritans, amplified by the thought of John Wesley and with an added, extreme confidence in the power of human action and will. Finney preached that people might achieve union with God in significant measure through their own action. Americans' determination to better themselves—materially, intellectually, and spiritually—moved their religious, political, and cultural impulses in ways characterized by both determined rationality and effusive optimism, methodological order and teleological enthusiasm. The results were not always good, indeed could bring community breakdown, self-destruction, and violence. Moreover, the passion for self-improvement could undermine the natural impetus toward community, especially at a time when the frontier beckoned, not just to families, but to individuals who would be trappers, Indian-fighters, and outlaws.

At roughly the same time as this awakening of the drive for self-improvement came a new challenge to American identity, especially in more urban areas. By 1850 2.2 million immigrants—10 percent of the entire population—resided in the United States. Not since the founding of the earliest, small and isolated colonies had such a high proportion of Americans been foreign-born. Moreover, while America always had had a significant amount of cultural, religious, and linguistic diversity, many of these new immigrants were more radically different from native-born Americans than their predecessors. Of particular concern were immigrants from Ireland, hundreds of thousands of whom were Catholic and most of whom were of impoverished and often uneducated peasant stock.

Catholics had been among America's earliest settlers. Maryland had been established as a haven for this most oppressed of English religious minorities—still, and for many decades, forbidden to openly practice their religion. But the small Catholic population was soon swamped by protestant settlers, who worked, at times, to marginalize them. Colonial Catholics maintained their faith but worked hard to take their place among mainstream Americans—including among patriots at the revolution. One prominent Catholic, John Carroll, signed the Declaration of Independence. Tocqueville remarked that, in his time, Catholics were public and enthusiastic in their support for American traditions and ideals.

Catholics, like most of those in this new wave of immigrants, were different from their predecessors. In part no doubt because of their sheer numbers, these immigrants often sought to maintain a separate culture, and remained in and worked to gain control over urban areas. Catholic immigrants were objects of special concern and suspicion because they worked to protect their children from protestant teachings in the public schools by setting up their own educational institutions. Protestant elites (as well as many of their followers) reacted with anger and something approaching panic. Catholicism, these protestants insisted, was "undemocratic." Catholics, they claimed, were blind followers of a Pope and Church hierarchy bent on world domination and therefore lacked the character of a free people and the loyalty of good citizens. Leading protestant figures demanded a governmental response to people they considered (wrongly, of course, and counter to many examples in history and in front of their very noses) dangerous to American souls and democratic institutions.

Protestant Americans had always borne some hostility toward Catholics, though Washington and many others had welcomed their support and participation in public life. Cultural hostility stiffened into political program in the face of significant immigration and, especially, Irish Catholic political organization. Protestant organizations and even a new political party (the American or "Know Nothing" Party) sought, with great success, to stymie Catholic attempts to gain local funding for parochial schools even as they insisted on continuing to teach from the (protestant) Bible in public schools. For the first time, mainstream figures began to demand a "separation of church and state"; in so doing, these figures set the stage for a political hostility toward religion they never intended. Then again, they were seeking to capitalize on a powerful phrase ("separation of church and state") that had been used frequently by more radical enlightenment thinkers such as Jefferson, though not to be found anywhere in the Constitution itself.

The battle over funding was damaging to cultural relations. Far more damaging, however, was the centralization of educational programming this fight brought about. Funding was centralized, at times at the state level, sapping local vitality and control. While most public schooling remained broadly protestant, a new ideology, most systematically set forth in the work of Massachusetts state legislator and head of the state board of education, Horace Mann, came to the fore. Mann instituted common standards, which spread especially through northern states, demanding secular "moral values" education, conformity in teacher training and curriculum, and bureaucratic control over all public schools. The result was hardly the kind of nationalization that characterized educational systems in much of Europe, but it began a trend of elite "professionalization," vapid secularization, and administrative centralization hostile to American self-government.

America had changed. Cities were taking on increased importance, bringing a transformation to the domestic economy and new ethnic and religious tensions. Slavery was more entrenched than ever, and a cause of increasing conflict. The frontier continued to beckon, more than ever encouraging migration, isolation, and a wild abandonment of civilization for the forests among the most adventurous. And, at the same time as a drive for self-improvement, a new class of cultural arbiters, professional educators, were asserting authority over schools throughout the nation.

How, then, did Americans remain American? For one thing, the trends we've noted did not dominate the lives of a still predominantly rural, self-governing people. Moreover, public life continued to be shaped by America's sturdy preexisting political structures, the pugnacious attachment of its people to their republican character, and above all a long tradition of administrative decentralization that fostered overlapping loyalties and conflicts. American political structures, emphasizing limitations on political power and fostering low-level conflict, helped maintain a pluralistic culture, characterized by multiple centers of authority; there was neither possibility nor need for any final "victor" in these conflicts. As a result, people were motivated, out of self-interest if nothing else, to maintain a modicum of civility with their opponents, such that even the relatively corrupt politics of the time could not fully undermine the American way of life.

Local sorting was crucial to public peace. Catholics founded their own towns on the frontier and formed their own neighborhoods in the cities. In the same way protestant sects had formed townships from the earliest settlements, so Catholics settled their own areas, making their own "deals" with one another and with neighboring communities to maintain their culture, even as they adapted to the requirements of settler life and the rough and tumble of American politics. Even as Catholics struggled against rules aimed at "assimilating" their children, they established schools and other local associations that maintained their essential way of life as they became American, even becoming a notable force in state and national public and political life.

True pluralism was built into the American landscape. In physical terms, America lacked any single political or cultural capital—Washington was new, unpleasant, and small and America's other cities were too isolated and relatively small to take all the attention and influence for themselves. In historical terms, Americans continued to live by the codes and habits they inherited from their ancestors, taking them along into the frontier. Even as Americans forged agreements for self-government in everything from new towns to wagon trains headed West, they refused to specify any code of laws. They were determined that "the law of God" was sufficient. In point of fact, they were not simply "making things up" as they went. Instead, they were relying on a common, broadly Christian vision of right and wrong, buttressed by long practice within their previous communities. In this way law and custom, even as later set down in common-law legal decisions, were left to adapt themselves to changing circumstances, but within a broad cultural consensus.

Law and the Constitution ruled because they were both omnipresent and invisible. The unruly people ruled itself through customs and norms or "habits of the heart" in Tocqueville's phrase. This people focused on its own way of life and self-conception central to its being. In Tocqueville's words:

> No idea was ever entertained of attacking the principle or contesting the rights of society; but the exercise of its authority was divided, in order that the office might be powerful and the officer insignificant, and that the community should be at once regulated and free. In no country in the world does the law hold so absolute a language as in America; and in no country is the right of applying it

vested in so many hands. The administrative power in the United States presents nothing either centralized or hierarchical in its constitution; this accounts
for its passing unperceived. The power exists, but its representative is nowhere
to be seen.[3]

Americans remained, decades after their political "founding" and centuries
after their first settlements, an unruly but law-abiding people. Their laws
remained strong because they were few and rooted in cultural consensus.
Before the age of administration, laws were admitted and followed when
what they forbade was bad in itself (*"mala in se"* in the lawyer's language)
and not wrong only on account of some statute written up for the convenience
of the rulers. Such a people would, in fact, regulate its own conduct, including
by setting forth rules forbidding mere "inconveniences" like the storing of
explosive gunpowder in highly populated areas. But such rules would be few
in number and consensual in origin. The unruly people was not an unregulated people, but it would regulate itself, and only when and to the extent it
deemed necessary for the public good.

NOTES

1. Alexis de Tocqueville, *Democracy in America*, trans. Phillips Bradley, vol. 1
(New York: Vintage, 1990), 61
  2. Ibid., 71.
  3. Ibid.

Chapter 10

American Women and the Power of Self-Sacrifice

Tocqueville famously credited the "singular prosperity and growing force" of the American people to "the superiority of its women."[1] His praise of American women stemmed from what he saw as their willing self-sacrifice. Women gave up the comforts of more civilized areas for settler life, often more than once in a lifetime. They brought culture in the form of books, music, religion, and their own habits. They took on many difficult and dangerous tasks within the household economy, all in service to husbands who held the legal right to control their property and represent the family to the outside world, and to the myriad children who took their time, attention, and often their health. Women held the household together. Confined to its domestic sphere, they reared children and held husbands to habits fostering self-governing virtues of piety, self-control, hard work, and self-sufficiency.

It would be a mistake, albeit an ideologically convenient mistake, to see these pioneer women as subservient drudges, mere tools in the hands of willful men. These women were shaped by traditions of settler life that required self-sufficiency and a species of Protestantism that emphasized each person's individual relationship with God. These traditions helped produce female leaders like Anne Hutchinson, the Puritan dissenter expelled from Boston for her radical preaching. Hutchinson continued preaching in Portsmouth, then moved to Long Island, where she was killed along with her family in an Indian massacre. American traditions also fostered entire sects that put equality before God into concrete practice. Quakerism flourished in America, with women preachers and women religious leaders who upheld the Quaker tradition of fearlessly proselytizing and willingly sacrificing their lives for their faith.

Tocqueville's praise of American women centered on how willingly they sacrificed—for religion and for their families. In an era, like today, in which we see few functioning families, in which "voluntary" is a term used only for the most radically self-chosen acts, such a claim may seem dishonest. But our forebears were not the individualists so many Americans strive to be today. There has been a change in our character away from local duties and toward individual demands for individual recognition and benefits. Whatever the demands of contemporary ideology and resentment, we can do justice to neither sex, nor to Americans as a people, by judging our forebears according to current standards. Here we can only spell out, briefly, the very different understanding, not only of women, but of men, children and above all the family, that characterized the American people, with decreasing vigor until quite recently.

The fountain of American life was the household. It was where Americans spent most of their time—whether farming the homestead, doing piecework for money, or rearing children. It was where Americans learned the virtues necessary for self-government. And it was the essential unit of American society. Heads of households joined in ruling their communities. But what was the household, how was it "ruled," and how did it organize the lives of its members?

Contemporary, individualist prejudices have trapped our perceptions of the household between the extremes of tyranny and chaos. But the American household was not held together by anything like the old Roman paterfamilias, the (male) absolute ruler who could literally kill other members in the interests of family honor. It also was far distant from the contemporary vision of interchangeable parts sharing employment and domestic duties while perhaps choosing to raise children (in cooperation with the government) until such time as divorce seems the most pleasant or convenient option. But the key distinctions for understanding the American household are those between it and England's aristocratic families.

As Tocqueville recognized, the American household was, most importantly, democratic. This did not mean any silly insistence on "voting" on all family matters. There were, as in all societies until sometime last week, male and female spheres—fighting, work in the fields, and heavy lifting for the men, work around the house and child-rearing for the women. The household was democratic principally in its not having an aristocratic structure. The key terms in England were entail and primogeniture. Under these legal practices, property was kept as much as possible in the hands of eldest sons. Inheritance laws forbade equal sharing of inherited land and wealth so that the patriarchal family could prosper, even if particular family members were left to the charity of eldest sons.

In America, the will of the testator (the dead fellow whose property was being handed on) ruled. Widows had a legal right to support for the rest of their lives. Custom encouraged protection for daughters and equal shares among sons. But the testator's will ruled. There was, then, real authority in the head of household, for he could disinherit vicious children. But children could and often did simply leave. The family itself was not the timeless, singular institution of England. Blood did not dictate one's place in society or in an organic whole demanding the kind of loyalty above all other loyalties one would find in an aristocratic House, where heritable royal power was the ultimate prize.

Some Borderlanders brought their clan loyalties with them to the United States. But the traditions that spawned blood feuds like the infamous one between the Hatfields and McCoys were distinctly backwoods phenomena, often more a warning than a commonplace. Constant movement to new lands meant that bonds between the generations, while real, were loose. The "nuclear" family of parents and children was often augmented by grandparents in the home, sibling neighbors, and ties of loyalty to more distant relations. But extended authority was limited; siblings were themselves heads of households and full participants in public life.

What did this mean for women? Perhaps most obviously, the arranged marriage was highly unusual in the United States. Girls (and boys) were not primarily chits in a game of family wealth and influence, so most chose (or at least could refuse) their mates. This was no small thing. And it brought with it significantly greater social freedom for girls and young women. Single women were not locked away from social interaction or even commercial life. Those convinced of early Americans' sexual repression might want to look up the term "bundling." Moreover, the lack of clear class distinctions meant that even most servant girls were free from the absolute rule of masters who might use them sexually without promise of marriage. Women who did not choose to marry had limited life choices. If they weren't from well-off families, single women generally had to enter specific professions, like schoolteaching or nursing, or go into factory work. But the choices were real and important, giving a self-governing dignity to those who made them.

Women also had somewhat greater rights to property ownership and commercial engagement in America than in Europe. In settler cultures, where husbands and fathers were often away or dead, this was a matter of commercial necessity. Women had to have real rights to buy, sell, and control property or the local economy might die. And, as would happen increasingly in later frontier territories like Montana and Wyoming, men who wished to attract more women to places where they were scarce found that granting them greater rights, including the right to vote, could be important for community survival. These factors had helped increase women's property rights in New England long before. Conditions allowed American women to show their strength, willingness to engage in hard work, ability to tame and rear children of good character, and civilizing influence in isolated homesteads; this garnered them a reputation for common sense and the capacity for self-rule. Settler townships demanded much of all members. Women in particular engaged in great self-sacrifice. But they did so willingly, pursuing new adventures and opportunities through hard work and grit, in effect holding a Bible (or child) in one hand and a pistol in the other.

NOTES

1. Alexis de Tocqueville, *Democracy in America*, trans. Phillips Bradley, vol. 2 (New York: Vintage, 1990), 214.

Chapter 11

Civil War

The Deals that Failed

Our purpose in this book is not to provide a comprehensive history of the United States. Rather, we seek to trace the American character through the changing circumstances that make up that history to see what has changed, what has stayed the same, and why. Our hope is that such a history will help Americans better understand the dilemmas we face today, in particular the seeming loss of our national identity and our conception of ourselves as a decent people whose traditions and way of life deserve to endure.

The Civil War strikes at the heart of Americans' self-conception as a self-governing and fundamentally decent people. It's tempting, then, to turn that struggle into a morality play among caricatures or, worse yet, a simple sign of the irretrievable evil of America and its people. Stipulating the clear evil of chattel slavery and of racism (moral enormities too common in the world even today), our goal here is not primarily to examine slavery itself. We seek instead to explain the impact of that institution. In doing so we also look at the status of the Constitution, our most important agreement among ourselves, before, during, and after the Civil War. That document was at issue throughout, and its uses during that struggle had consequences that remain with us to this day.

Americans in general were, of course, racists. Racism has been well-nigh universal throughout human history. The ancient Greeks termed all foreigners "barbarians"—beings who speak unintelligibly, such that "bar-bar" was all a Greek heard—who deserved enslavement. The Han Chinese held in contempt "lesser" groups within China, referring to non-Asians as "barbarians" or "devils." Muslims in Mauritania, Niger, and Sudan, among other countries today, hold Black Africans in slavery. In sum, humans tend to denigrate those outside their own group, especially if they look and sound different from themselves. Historically, this has allowed groups (whether defined by skin color, religion, culture, language, or some other characteristic) to justify their own selfish conduct, taking others' goods, land, and even persons for their own use.

Slavery during the eighteenth and nineteenth centuries was a common global phenomenon. Most African ("black") slaves were imported into America through thriving African slave markets. At this same time Europeans ("whites") could find themselves captured by pirates in the Mediterranean and sold into slavery in North Africa or the Middle East. Still, the combination of racism and race-based servitude within a constitutional republic proved particularly damaging in the United States.

British colonists brought a specific form of human bondage with them to the New World, namely indentured servitude. In exchange for free passage (or on account of criminal conviction in Britain), many settlers were obliged to serve a term of years as unpaid laborers. But the duties of indentured servants were bound by law. Large-scale race-based chattel slavery, the often-absolute dominion of one human being over another, was imported from Caribbean colonies near the end of the seventeenth century. It proved unprofitable (as well as morally repugnant) in most of the North, where mass agricultural labor was not practicable. Slowly, slavery died out in New England, even as it gained ground on Southern plantations. By the time of the Constitution's drafting, what was then the independent nation of Vermont had passed a law freeing slaves when they turned twenty-one and slavery had been banned in the Northwest Territory (what would become the states of the Upper Midwest). Right up to the Civil War, slavery continued to be pushed southward out of the North. This trend deeply concerned Deep South slave-holders who, a minority in their own states, feared increased slave unrest, loss of influence over national politics, and "invasion" of their border states by troublesome free whites.

The Constitution was written with a view of slavery as an aberration. English common law never had allowed for the actual ownership and total control of one person by another. In England and America slavery was allowed only because and to the extent it was supported by specific, enacted, positive laws. By forbidding congressional action against the slave trade only until 1808 and by refusing to affirmatively approve chattel slavery, the Constitution looked forward to a time when state support of this institution, hated by many revolutionary leaders, would end and so end slavery itself.

Unfortunately, the Constitution's ratification was made possible only by inclusion of a corrupt bargain—a deal by which slaves were counted as three-fifths of a person, thus increasing the representation of slaveholding states in Congress. Non-slaveholding states also agreed to imposition of federal laws empowering slave catchers to operate in their lands, forcing local officials to assist them in kidnapping presumed escapees from bondage and punishing anyone who dared shield the accused. In addition, the

Constitution's ambiguity regarding the status of slave ownership in federal territories empowered an increasingly small number of large slaveholders to control, unsettle, and finally break the conditions of peace within the republic.

Even in most of the plantation-dominated Deep South, fewer than half of white families owned slaves and less than half the population was enslaved (though South Carolina was majority slave by 1820 and a few other states became majority slave later). Slave and slaveholder numbers were much smaller in the "Upper" South, and even smaller in border states, approaching the vanishing point in Delaware. Moreover, the South was no cultural monolith. Borderlanders and their descendants were common, along with their unruliness, their rural settlement patterns, and their preference for subsistence farming as the way of life. This was not the case, however, in ethnically diverse Louisiana, or in the upper echelons of society—the "slavocracy" dominated by descendants of Caribbean immigrant slaveholders whose plantations (like those of large slaveholders in general) were, in effect, small towns and who aspired to rule. The slavocracy's cultural position, along with compromised law and politics, gave them outsized influence such that they expected to have their way on the slavery issue and every political issue even peripherally associated with it. For decades, this small planter class (which included some few Borderlanders and other non-Caribbean immigrants) succeeded in manipulating party politics and intersectional hostility to buttress slavery's status within the union.

It would be foolish to attribute these developments to power politics, or even to Southern pride alone. Right up to the beginning of the bloodletting, parties on both sides attempted to make deals to prevent secession and war. But slavery encouraged arrogance, wounded pride, and fear among slaveholders as it encouraged resentment and worry over the potential loss of natural rights among white men in non-slaveholding sections, festering into a deep cultural hostility. Northerners developed a habit of castigating Southerners for slavery, even as they instituted their own racist laws and made clear their own desire that the Africans in their midst be made to disappear from America. Southerners, including non-slaveholders, responded with rage, fear of Northern aggression, and something approaching terror of possible slave insurrections and/or murder of their overlords. With some interparty debate, most Southern states moved to stifle discussion of slavery's morality through congressional "gag" rules, state suppression of free speech, and officially sanctioned mob action.

But slaveholders were far from the only powerful political force active in the South. For most of this era there was a two-party system in the region, with Whigs opposing many of the more draconian measures championed by Democrats. Moreover, non-slaveholding Southerners were no mere puppets of aristocratic rulers. With the only partial exception of South Carolina, white males had the vote throughout the South and the majority Borderlanders out-side the few urban areas were not deferential to their "betters"—though many poor landowners often looked toward becoming large, slaveholding landown-ers themselves someday. Upcountry in the Carolinas, in northern Alabama, and throughout the mountainous border regions in particular, slavery was tolerated at best and secession an unpopular cause. But regional tensions undermined the power of such substantial minorities as Civil War approached and slaveowners flexed their political muscle.

In the name of self-government, then, slaveholding forces undermined the bases of republican government in freedom of speech and assembly, even as they worked to undermine states' rights through increasingly oppressive fed-eral Fugitive Slave laws. The federal courts, sadly, were extreme supporters of this system, bending fact, law, and Constitution in their drive to "protect property" in defiance of traditional legal and moral limitations on power. Eventually, further deals became impossible because, whatever the deep flaws on the side of the North (and slaveholding border states, which stayed in the Union) too many Southerners had come to see their region in terms irreconcilable to self-government within a constitutional republic established for a free people. Northerners saw compromises regarding slavery as tempo-rary stopgaps to prevent a last flood before slavery subsided. Meanwhile, a significant number of powerful Southerners, having come to see slavery as a positive good, sought to redraw the Constitution itself to grant equal consti-tutional and even social status to slavery. When it became clear that the slave power (as it had come to be called in the North) could no longer dominate national politics, Deep South slaveholders chose secession, bringing most (though far from all) Southerners with them.

Troubles between the sections began before the republic, as evidenced by the necessity of a "three-fifths rule" to secure constitutional ratification. Such troubles were exacerbated by America's westward expansion. Would new states be slave or free? Southern slaveholders demanded recognition of the equal right of slaveholders to establish their "peculiar" institution within new territories and potential states. Northerners, fearing increased slaveholding power and desiring that slavery (and Africans themselves) be kept out of new lands, balked.

The first major attempt to address these disputes was the Missouri Compromise of 1820. It drew a line through the territorial map representing Jefferson's then-recent Louisiana Purchase, with slavery to be legal below it and illegal above. Missouri would be the (slaveholding) exception. It seemed there always would be exceptions to undermine each new deal.

The next major deal was made necessary by the 1846–1848 war with Mexico—a war one of the two major parties (the Whigs) opposed in large part because it would unsettle the Missouri Compromise. Four years of raucous debate, focused as much on honor and pride as political advantage, ensued over whether and how far slavery would extend westward into territory seized from Mexico. The Compromise of 1850 involved a series of laws setting the borders of the new slave state of Texas, dividing up other territories among free and undetermined jurisdictions, banning the slave trade in the District of Columbia, and establishing a new Fugitive Slave Law that placed the thumb of injustice on the scale to favor slaveholders in court.

Both sides were unhappy with the Compromise of 1850. That deal made clear slavery's limited range as a viable option in the West even as it imposed a legal regime that subordinated the rights of states and their citizens to federal rules aimed at empowering slave catchers. Belligerence at times broke out into violence. Especially harmful were the massive, coercive voter fraud, lynchings, and bushwhackings (instigated by both sides) in "Bleeding Kansas." The 1854 Kansas-Nebraska Act, yet another new deal, had opened Kansas as a potential slaveholding state, but helped not at all.

At this point the Supreme Court, acting for the first time as a grand super-legislature, stepped in to make matters much worse.

Dred Scott v. Sandford[1] remains the most damaging Supreme Court decision in American history. It was seen by the judges who handed down the opinion (and by the future failed president James Buchanan, who worked behind the scenes to influence it) as a means to save the Union by putting the slavery issue to rest, once and for all. It instituted a form of judicial lawmaking, in defiance of the Constitution's clear intent, that helped bring Civil War and perverts judicial decision-making to this day.

Scott was a slave who sued for his freedom on the grounds that his owners, having taken him to free territory before returning him to a slaveholding jurisdiction, had thereby forfeited ownership rights in him. There was ample precedent for Scott's claim stretching back decades in the United States and Great Britain. Chief Justice Roger Taney, writing the court's majority opinion, sought to nullify the very foundations of these precedents by holding that black African slaves and their descendants were never intended to be included under the word "citizens" in the American Constitution.

Slave or free, according to Taney, people of African descent, since well before American independence, had "been regarded as beings of an inferior order, and altogether unfit to associate with the white race, either in social or political relations; and so far inferior, that they had no rights which the white man was bound to respect." No federal rights, privileges, or immunities, including the right to sue as Scott was attempting, could exist for such a subject people. Not even African Americans' state-granted rights, which had been the subject of repeated litigation over many decades, could stand in the face of Taney's sweeping, ahistorical decision.

Up to this time, states had been free to define and enforce citizenship according to local rules and procedures. In some states freedmen had voted on the very question whether to ratify the Constitution. Yet Taney declared a national prohibition against citizenship for anyone of African descent. And Taney was not satisfied with this illogical and counter-traditional misreading of citizenship's requirements. The bulk of his opinion takes aim at federal policies in the territories, undoing decades of hard-won political compromise, in direct opposition to the plain meaning of the Constitution. Taney asserted that only territories already owned by the United States at the time of the Constitution's drafting (i.e., the Northwest Territory) were subject to congressional regulation. This meant that subsequent regulation—the Missouri Compromise—was unconstitutional. Henceforth, slavery would be constitutionally protected in all territories and, indeed, in every state in the Union, whatever the wishes of each state's people.

In defense of slavery Taney formulated a theory of judicial supremacy over the law and plain meaning of the Constitution that corrupts our courts to this day. Here he looked to the Fifth Amendment, protecting citizens from being deprived of "life, liberty, or property without due process of law." Because slaves were property, Taney claimed, they could not be "taken" from any citizen merely because he had transported his slave "property" into a federal territory where slavery happened to be illegal. As Taney put it: "an act of Congress which deprives a citizen of the United States of his liberty or property, merely because he came himself or brought his property into a particular Territory of the United States, and who had committed no offence against the laws, could hardly be dignified with the name of due process of law."

On the surface, Taney's due process argument might make sense: it would be unfair to punish someone, including by seizing their property, if he broke no law. Therefore, to take Scott away from his owner when there was no law specifically barring anyone from bringing his slave into the jurisdiction would be an act of mere power, not law. But this was not the situation. From the beginning, in England, the United States, and Missouri itself, it had been understood that slavery is by nature illegal and so made legal only by positive law. Thus, wherever that positive law was missing, there could be no slavery, hence no right to hold someone in slavery.

Taney's cry of "unfair" is that of a lawgiver, not a judge. Rejecting his legal duty, and the character demanded of a judge, he assumed the authority and power to wipe away the long-standing law on slavery in the American tradition. He used the unfortunate fact of racial prejudice as cover to strike down decades worth of law, constitutional compromise, and state action fully in keeping with America's common law and constitutional traditions. All in the name of "settling" the slavery issue forever.

It was all for less than nothing. The *Dred Scott* decision inflamed Northern fears of the slave power even as it encouraged slaveholders to demand further changes to guarantee equal treatment and status for their institution. It undercut the prestige of the court and blew up the Missouri Compromise, leaving future combatants with no clear basis for any new deal. In the end, not even incoming President Lincoln's agreement to a proposed constitutional amendment guaranteeing slavery's perpetual protection in all states in which it then was allowed could prevent secession. The Lower South stood on Taney's shoulders and demanded a fundamentally transformed Constitution with federal protections for nationwide slaveholder rights. This free states could not allow, for it would undermine their own self-governance. South Carolina seceded, a few states followed, South Carolina attacked Fort Sumter and, when the Union prepared to respond, war ensued.

Did slavery change the American character materially and/or permanently? Almost. Attitudes toward slavery varied over time and space, even within the South. Twice Virginia came close to abandoning the institution, first at the revolution, then in 1832 in the aftermath of Nat Turner's slave rebellion. But slavery, while at the root of the problem, still was only a part of that problem; its consequences in culture and law posed great dangers on their own to both the Union and the American character. Culturally, slavery made racism more relevant and toxic in America because it brought more Africans to its shores in a condition of degrading servitude that also effectively made them competitors for "white" jobs and land. For many decades, persons and communities on both sides of the racial divide would operate within an atmosphere of distrust, resentment, and even hatred. There was also, of course, the corrupting influence of power. Countless observers have noted the tendency of absolute power to corrupt its holders; thus, the immense but fragile pride of slaveholders in particular that caused so many demands, threats, and finally, secession.

This is not to say that all conceptions of honor are dangerous. Virtue and the drive to practice (and be recognized for it) are crucial to a free people. Relevant, reality-based norms of right conduct and concern for one's reputation are essential for any people and produced many great men and acts in the United States. The mere name "George Washington" makes our point. But diverging conceptions of honor and a distinctly antidemocratic code among slaveholders poisoned public discourse during this era, indicating at least the beginnings of a separate culture hostile to the mainstream of the American tradition and character.

The most telling example, here, is provided by South Carolina Congressman Preston Brooks. Brooks, a wealthy slaveowner, took offense at a speech given on the floor of the Senate by Massachusetts' Charles Sumner. In May of 1856, Sumner had disparaged slaveowners in general and Brooks's relative

Senator Andrew Butler in particular, in a long, angry speech criticizing the Kansas-Nebraska Act. Sumner violently condemned his opponents' actions and character, going so far as to accuse Butler of sexually exploiting his slaves and mocking Butler's stroke-induced speech slurring. The speech was incendiary and insulting.[2]

Brooks determined to avenge his family honor upon Sumner. The traditional manner of seeking such "satisfaction" had long been the duel. But Brooks was (rather conveniently) advised by intimates that Sumner was unworthy of such "gentlemanly" treatment and so instead should be given a public beating. For two days Brooks shadowed Sumner but failed to find him in a sufficiently vulnerable position for him to safely attack the larger, stronger man, so, with two fellow Southern congressmen, he came upon Sumner on the Senate floor. Announcing to the seated Sumner that his speech had been a "libel," Brooks proceeded to beat him on the head with a heavy, gold-topped cane, striking him repeatedly where he sat, then following him and striking him more as Sumner pulled himself up using his bolted-down desk, stumbled away, and tried to defend himself while Brooks's friends sought to prevent any outside interference. Brooks, who broke his cane while beating Sumner, received several thousand new ones from Southern supporters; he received only a small fine as punishment for his act, which incapacitated Sumner for several years.

Brooks and his friends made no pretense of seeking any kind of "fair fight," for they proclaimed Sumner unworthy of consideration as a gentleman. Further, while Northerners condemned the attack for using brutality to stifle debate, Southerners praised Brooks, and his constituents returned him to Congress. Americans' code of honor had led President Jackson into numerous duels. In its pseudo-aristocratic, Southern version it now precluded such niceties in favor of public beatings. The origins of such mutations of honor in the slaveholders' ability (and "right") to beat their bound slaves are obvious. That they now would extend this "right" to beating members of the United States Senate, within the chamber itself, shows the level of separation some slaveholders now accorded themselves from standards of conduct applicable to the generality of their fellow Americans. The honor of the South, as of aristocratic slaveowners, trumped the needs of republican government. Violence and brutality were common in the United States and are so throughout the world to this day. But not all Americans, not all Southerners, tied fair treatment so clearly to status. Brooks and his supporters felt that "gentlemen" were excused from the basic democratic principle of fair play in dealing with their "inferiors."

Such arrogance and hatred underlay atrocities during the Civil War when, for example, Confederate soldiers after several battles slaughtered Black Union soldiers. Still, there was another, far more positive side to Southern honor, which was active even during the Civil War. This honor was most apparent in the figure and conduct of Confederate General Robert E. Lee. A traditional Southern slaveholder, Lee rejected the notion that slavery was a positive good, though he had provided for manumission of his own slaves only upon his death. Like many Southerners outside the Caribbean clique, Lee had opposed secession but felt compelled to defend his native Virginia when its rights were put at risk. He joined the secession when, in response to South Carolina's attack on Fort Sumter, President Lincoln sought, without congressional approval, to commandeer Virginia's (and other states') militias for military action against seceding states. After years of vicious war, it was Lee who determined not merely to surrender his troops, but to insist that they not engage in further guerrilla resistance to the Union. Beloved by his men, his plea for peace was, for the time, heeded and he worked for the rest of his life to heal the wounds of civil war.

Honor was not, even in the South, simply a selfish, prideful impulse fomenting war. It was, rather, an aspect of American character capable of producing great virtue and, when corrupted, acts of brutal arrogance. The same might be said of that core American norm, self-government.

From fugitive slave laws to nationalized protections for slavery, to oppressive laws and illegal actions aimed at stifling public debate, powerful slaveowners justified anti-republican and nationalizing laws as necessary to prevent "interference" with the South's "peculiar institution." Such hypocritical claims to defend self-government were successful for many years because of cultural hostility and the mistaken notion that a section of the country—the Deep South—could be self-governing in the same way as a state or a nation. In the end, misplaced loyalty to a collection of states allowed powerful secessionist slaveholders in a few states to manipulate a larger number of states to join in secession.

American self-government always has been a complicated idea and practice. As persons, communities, and states Americans have held loyalties deeper than that to the distant, limited federal government. Creation of a separate, sectional identity rooted in human bondage never fully took hold before, during, or after the Civil War. Wide swaths of the Southern populace rejected it, even as some of them supported the Confederacy in the name of states' right to secede from any larger union at will. But the fact that the natural coalescence of loyalties from shared ethnic ancestry, rural settlement patterns, and predominantly agricultural ways could be cobbled together into a secessionist section shows how loyalties to groups, sections, or ideologies can undermine loyalty to both one's natural associations and to the nation (and people) that fosters and protects them.

This is not to say that secession is always and everywhere treasonous or even a bad idea. Indeed, it had been threatened more than once in American history and was suggested by slavery abolitionists themselves as a means of separating slavery from America's constitutional republicanism. Moreover, problems of distance and scale—of too many people over too great a distance for proper governance—or the breakdown of cultural consensus may make secession the only means by which self-government can survive. Once there are two people rather than one, secession becomes a matter of convenience rather than moral absolutes—as the Declaration of Independence makes clear. The nation is not, after all, the repository of a people's virtue, but rather a means by which a people may maintain peace among its fundamental associations while defending itself from potential aggressors. The problem of Civil War secession lay in the slavocracy's insistence that its will would rule, either over the entire nation or over other Southern states sharing only some of its culture and norms.

Despite the best efforts of gentlemen like Lee, as well as Lincoln and others who sought national healing, hostilities, including racism, that produced the Civil War were if anything exacerbated by that bloody conflict and its aftermath. What made matters worse was the unconstitutional thinking that helped bring war through the *Dred Scott* decision. Stripped of any rights, privileges, or immunities of citizenships, freed slaves were left without the means to defend themselves in the hostile atmosphere of the postwar South. Forced to look to Northern troops and a few "carpetbaggers" and local men of integrity, freed slaves and their descendants were abandoned at the end of Reconstruction, without the procedural rights, explicitly promised in the Constitution, necessary to make real the more abstract promises of democratic equality. To this tragedy we turn next.

NOTES

1. 60 U.S. (19 How.) 393 (1857).

2. Not, however, uniquely insulting. Butler earlier had made his own insulting and sexually and racially charged remarks regarding Sumner but at this time was away from Congress recuperating.

Chapter 12

Aftermath

Salvaging the Deal, or Replacing It?

Southerners were the aggressors in the Civil War. But they were not just bullies or crazy people. Secessionist leaders, especially but not exclusively the large slaveholders, were genuinely afraid of slave insurrections and northern hostility. This fear was not irrational, though it was based on relatively minor political losses and the actions of a tiny number of abolitionists, revolting slaves, and supporters of John Brown's assault on Harpers Ferry. It rested also on a more general fear that slavery, the institution most though far from all Southerners admitted was intrinsically wrong, would flame out in violence, taking with it their way of life.

Slavery's precarious state was highlighted by the attempt to negotiate a constitutional settlement without war. In particular, Deep South partisans rejected an amendment to protect slavery in perpetuity wherever it was already legal. They did so for the same reason President Lincoln was willing to support it: because in the long run it wouldn't make any difference. Both sides were convinced that, if relegated to its original jurisdictions, without additional constitutional aids, slavery would die.

Lincoln's conviction on this issue doubtless contributed to his determination *not* to prosecute the Civil War as a war for liberation. He was aggressive—calling up militia in Southern states immediately after the attack on Fort Sumter (an act of dubious constitutionality that pushed the Upper South into the arms of the Confederacy), refusing to call Congress back in session for several months as he took unilateral military action, and taking extraconstitutional steps like suspending the writ of habeas corpus. But these actions were all aimed at saving the Union as he perceived it, period. Lincoln argued that he was acting according to a higher law in seeking to salvage the Constitution in its full territorial extent—to include the states of the Deep South (as well as the opening West). His goal was a more united nation, loyal to a federal government that would act vigorously to expand its territory and centralize its powers through public works and other programs forging a more national economy. Whatever one thinks of these goals, they were not instituted with the purpose of bringing social transformation through racial equality.

The South's military effectiveness and Union generals' lackluster performance extended the war. Eventually Lincoln saw the advantage of emancipating slaves within Confederate territory to weaken the South's ability to fight. His Emancipation Proclamation also answered Northerners' increased demands to stamp out the unjust institution identified with Southern arrogance and disloyalty. Yet Lincoln himself refused to treat the Civil War as one of true rebellion. Rather, he sought to restore the United States as closely as possible to the former status quo, except that federal supremacy would now be fully active and respected.

Victory required emancipation. The bravery and loyalty of African Americans combined with the Emancipation Proclamation to create a feeling of indebtedness, a belated (and for many still sadly partial) recognition of Africans' humanity, and a determination to eliminate the social structures underlying rebellion to make slavery's end inescapable. But emancipation was not enough to secure real, American freedom. The Constitution and American character both demanded local self-government. Unfortunately, most white people in the South defined self-government as white government. What, then, was to be done?

Lincoln barely began his attempt to reconcile the South, which entailed limited loyalty oaths and minimal reforms in exchange for reentry into full rights within the Union, when he was assassinated. His successor, Andrew Johnson, held Africans of all kinds in extreme, open contempt and sought to keep them subservient to whites. He handed out wholesale pardons of southern leaders that short-circuited any systematic reckoning with the power relations of slavery even as former slaves sought to make a place for themselves in a changed world.

Post–Civil War conditions in the South were chaotic. About four million men, women, and children were freed by the Thirteenth Amendment. Slaves (or "serfs") have been freed in many times and places; disorder is inevitable. Masses of impoverished, usually uneducated, and understandably resentful people are set free from angry former masters, themselves facing financial disaster, hurting for labor, and unwilling to treat former slaves as fully human. In the United States the situation was made worse because slavery was race-based, marking freedmen out as part of a hated class.

Great numbers of freedmen set out at once to find work, family members torn from them under slavery, and the makings of a decent life. Multitudes of desperately poor people hit the road, homeless among hate- and fear-filled whites who wanted nothing so much as a return to prewar conditions. Johnson responded by imposing a military rule upholding black codes that stripped freedmen of basic rights and recommitted them to plantation life.

It wasn't until after Johnson left office that Republicans in Congress were able to use Union troops to provide real protections and oversight. They acted on two fronts, the constitutional and the social/political. Congress worked to bring freedmen into America's constitutional order by amending the Constitution to guarantee their fundamental rights. They also worked to bring freedmen fully into American public life as part of its self-governing citizenry. They took concrete action on the constitutional front, but its effectiveness was severely undermined by political and social failure.

Despite their prejudices, Republicans in Congress sought to secure for freedmen the fundamental rights of American citizenship: life, liberty, and property. The last of these has caused the most confusion. Property, often expanded rhetorically as "the pursuit of happiness," had been central to American conceptions of a good life since before the Revolution. The revolutionaries had referenced it in public arguments, appeals, and state charters of rights because they recognized how essential property is to securing life itself, as well as liberty and any possibility for happiness. Property is essential to making a living—especially by working the land but also through ownership of one's own tools and/or labor. And the right to property is essential to making deals with other people over labor, livestock, and the other goods of commercial and domestic life.

Americans have never apologized for our basic materialism. We have, in fact, seen it as a safe, reasonable response to the inevitable dangers of life to tend to our own business. But slaves have no business to attend to; they are treated as part of the business of their owners. Republicans in Congress recognized that freedmen had to have the right to own property, to enter contracts, and to defend their rights in court if their lives, physical liberty, and ability to gain self-sufficiency were to be defensible. Unfortunately, the southern plantation economy demanded unskilled, compliant laborers working for a bare subsistence without hope of future improvement. Conflict ensued, and Congress, after passing some ineffective civil rights legislation, pushed successfully for the Fourteenth Amendment, which required that all states recognize freedmen's equal right to life, liberty, and property, and such other privileges and immunities as the states chose to recognize in their white citizens. They then pushed for the Fifteenth Amendment in the vain hope that the right to vote might be enough to empower freedmen to defend, at the state and local level, rights recognized at the distant, federal level.

The constitutional deal would not be changed, only expanded to include freedmen. Republicans saw these protections as everything a man could and should ask for—essentially the means to make his own way in the world. The protections failed because they applied only to the states and not to the significant number of people (and not only in the South) who continued to deny African Americans' full humanity. Intimidation, violence, and lynching were repeatedly visited upon freedmen who sought to exercise their rights and, even where prosecutions occurred, judges and juries sided with whites against clear law and evidence. "Jury nullification" always has been a problem for Americans; prejudice sometimes blinds people to the truth and to their duty so that they punish the innocent and let the guilty go free regardless of what the law dictates. Unfortunately, on account of rational fear, issues of political power, and simple race hatred, administrative abuse and jury nullification became so common in some areas that law ceased to rule where the rights of freedmen were at issue. Law, and even constitutional amendment, in the end depends on the people's basic virtue or decency; if people do not recognize a moral duty to uphold the law as written against their own or the community's prejudices, law becomes powerless.

Why didn't the North force the issue—demand, if necessary at the point of a gun, that white southerners respect the rights of the freedmen? The North did some of this through the Freedmen's Bureau and through Enforcement Acts that relied on Union soldiers. But the attempt was limited by northern impatience, ambivalence, and limited resources. The ambivalence was not just on account of racism. The problem was intrinsically difficult: how does one act against the majority of a population, or even against a relatively small minority if the majority refuses to cooperate? Such problems have faced colonial powers, conquering nations, and victors in various civil wars from time immemorial. The usual answer is tyranny, land confiscation, and mass bloodshed.

Johnson's mass pardons made a second conquest of the South impossible and there was little stomach for it in any event. The lack of bloodlust is obviously a good thing. Many nations suffer for centuries from violent hatreds spawned in civil wars' bloody reprisals, ethnic cleansings, and even genocide. The reason for the relative decency of Northern behavior lies in development of our constitutional tradition. To "undo" pardons was unthinkable. To rule endlessly from Washington was equally unthinkable.

Moreover, the Civil War itself was fought over a genuinely contested issue: whether the states had in fact broken the deal, violated the constitution, by seceding. Various states, including in the North, had threatened secession long before 1861 and the argument had enjoyed significant, sustained support. Long-standing state loyalties were a factor, here, as was the generally recognized fact that the federal government was derivative; it had been granted only specific, enumerated powers by a constitution that was ratified by conventions held within and voting for states.

Slavery alone made the Southern cause immoral in most eyes. And slavery was definitively ended by the Thirteenth Amendment. What else, then, must be done with the rebellious South? The answer attempted in the United States was Reconstruction. The southern states were to be "reconstructed" through federally mandated local laws and state constitutional provisions to make them worthy of full reentry into the Union. The problem with this program from the start was that Congress could never agree on just what southern states must do before regaining full rights. As important, Congress was unwilling to change the nature of the constitutional deal by taking on a fundamentally transformative role. Unlike today, Americans of the time were not willing to use the federal government to force people to treat one another fairly. Respecting the fundamental character of the Constitution as an agreement among states, they refused to destroy local self-government in the name of fundamental fairness. Only the states had the police power, and that was how it would stay after a brief, in the end unsuccessful, attempt to reconstruct local judicial administration.

The freedmen would not have federal support for long. What they had was the vote. And they used it to gain, for a time, significant political influence. Reconstruction governments were only in power for about a decade (the time frame varied by state but centered on the late 1860s to late 1870s). And they were not "run" by freedmen. Almost all high state officials were white—either recent immigrants from the North ("carpetbaggers") or whites who had remained loyal to the Union ("scalawags"). But freedmen were well represented in most southern state legislatures during this era.

Resistance was extreme, violent, and coordinated from among the (often majority) part of the population disenfranchised on account of service to the Confederacy. Reconstruction governments at the time were portrayed as hopelessly corrupt and incompetent, which further added to the view that freedmen simply couldn't govern themselves. The unfairness of this charge must be understood in context. Reconstruction governments were all Republican. And the Republican Party—the Party of Lincoln—was in crucial ways merely a successor to the Whigs—the party of Lincoln's political hero, Henry Clay.

Republicans were inheritors of a political party dedicated to nationalism and a relatively expansive understanding of the Constitution. They sought increased political integration and an extensive program of "internal improvements" controlled by the federal government. For decades the Whigs had tried but failed to supplant the Democrats as America's dominant party. In Lincoln they found the powerful president they had always lacked. In the Civil War they found the great, unifying cause denied them by America's expansive, varied, and decentralized nature. In victory over rebellion and slavery they found a means to delegitimize that decentralization, along with concern for state's rights, limited government, and the Democratic Party itself. The result was a prolonged period of social, economic, and political centralization that spawned massive corruption but failed to make real the promises of the post-war constitutional settlement, especially for African Americans.

These policies would bring great change to the North—solidifying national markets, encouraging mass industrial development, bankrupting countless farmers, forcing men into a new, industrial urban workforce, and ushering in the era of the railroads—of great concentrations of wealth and government corruption. We turn to these issues in a later chapter. Here it is most important to emphasize what they also brought to the South: bankruptcy. Unlike northern states, those in the South were without funds after the Civil War. In a time of economic depression, with land values in the cellar, tax money almost nonexistent, tens of thousands of veterans home from the war without pay, the old Confederate money useless, and vast destruction across the land, southern state governments simply hadn't the funds for public works.

But Reconstruction governments chose to follow the Republican party platform and spend massive amounts of money subsidizing railroads (many of which went bankrupt), starting a system of universal education essentially from scratch, and attempting, in a time of voluntary legislative service, to pay legislators a full-time wage. Corruption followed in the South as in the North. But its consequences in the South were catastrophic.

Public education had never been a priority in the South. Now it was being extended to freedmen whom many southerners didn't want educated. Land had never been taxed much in the South. Now the old aristocracy was to be taxed at a time when its members already were going bankrupt. And railroads had never been a priority in the South. Now state governments sought to catch up with the same massive subsidies as in the North. This last policy proved especially disastrous, not just because it brought massive corruption, but because it destroyed an essential part of the Reconstruction coalition in the South, the so-called scalawags. This group of loyal Union supporters were mostly yeoman farmers determined to maintain their traditional, American way of life independent of the plantations. Unfortunately, railroad expansion exposed them to international markets, pressuring them to leave off subsistence farming for cash crops. Thousands lost their farms, their independence, and their ability to fight for Reconstruction.

The problems of corruption and railroad subsidies that produced little save dislocation for the yeomanry were the same throughout the Republican United States during this era. But the combination of dire poverty, greater cultural resistance to nationalization, and racism contributed to the breakdown of post–Civil War coalitions and the rise of "redeemer" political movements. These movements, generally headed by the former planter class or its merchant allies, often cooperated in race-based violence that killed thousands. On occasion the federal government would intervene, sometimes with significant success, but there was little stomach for a fight that went on for years.

Reconstruction petered out, especially as Northern troops were siphoned off to break strikes in Northern industrial areas and fight Indians aroused to violence by the invasion of aggressive, subsidized railroads.

We aren't trying to argue for some utopian vision of the past: "if only the North had done x everything would have been fine." There was no such magic bullet; governments rarely bring freedom with bullets. The freedmen suffered greatly in the aftermath of Reconstruction as openly racist policies, including the infamous Jim Crow segregation laws, were instituted and economic opportunity vanished. White yeoman farmers suffered as well. Their way of life was swallowed up by a corrupt form of plantation rule. Sharecropping was less bad than some recent alternatives, but, buttressed as it was by a draconian system of debt servitude, it trapped millions of whites and blacks. Others—white people and freedmen both—withdrew into the hills to swear off engagement with the wider world.

In the decades that followed, freedmen and their descendants did a remarkable job of restoring family and community life within the confines of segregation. They had worked for a very American dream: life, liberty, and property within self-governing communities. It was taken from them by a corrupt and dying elite in an atmosphere of hatred and fear. Against a resurgent planter class and against the trials of a new age, white people as well as freedmen in the South would work to maintain the yeoman life central to the American way. In often tragic fashion they remained an unruly people.

Chapter 13

The West

Why couldn't the North enforce Reconstruction? In large part because they didn't have enough troops. And why didn't they have enough troops? In large part because too many of them were on the western frontier fighting Indians. Why?

As ever, American settlers after the Civil War were hungry for new land to the point where many squatted and some even seized land where they thought they could get away with it. Conflict between a growing, restless, and land-hungry people with a native population of only 250,000 Indians claiming dominion over half a continent was inevitable. But the speed and intensity of the conflict made it impossible for any decent and humane result, or for an even vaguely just deal to be struck.

And why was western settlement in the late nineteenth century so fast and intense? Government policy. As happened far too often, misguided and corrupt politics brought out the dark side of American character, fomenting violence and lawlessness. Still, where in other countries ruling classes imposed static squalor and subjection on people in even newly settled areas, among Americans an inner core of resiliency, vigor, and habits of local cooperation helped bring a yeoman's order and rough justice out of chaos.

President Polk's war with Mexico (1846–1848) had vastly expanded American territory and unsettled the slavery question. It also extended Americans' reach to the Pacific coast, with its vast trading possibilities and soon-discovered gold, silver, and copper. For years the West's potential wealth went largely untapped because it lay on the other side of a vast, "empty" area of tribal rule and untracked wilderness. There grew, then, a feeling of lost opportunity and a relentless drive to reach out from East to West.

Americans had always been driven to spread and multiply. But up until the Civil War era they hadn't pursued grand, government-funded projects aimed at making it happen. Jefferson's Louisiana Purchase, which more than doubled the size of the early republic, had created its own problems of a distant frontier. New Orleans is over 1,300 miles from New York City. Rivers were nonexistent or impassable for much of the way and there were no roads. Yet early talk of extending the only decent, long road in America—the National Road that stretched from the Potomac to the Ohio rivers—went nowhere. This road was specifically provided for in the Constitution as a post road (designed to carry the mail). Constitutionally speaking, it could have been extended to New Orleans. But the federal government was weak and poor. It had taken twenty-six years to build the National Road and Americans were too busy moving on their own to stop and ask for help from a federal government they distrusted in any event.

Americans constantly fought over internal improvements and the taxes needed to pay for them. Almost all public works (the Erie Canal was perhaps the largest of all during this era) were undertaken at the state level. And well before the Civil War states had begun subsidizing local railroad lines. But plans for a federal scheme ran aground on principled opposition to federal interference and, more important, competition for routes. Every senator and representative wanted the railroad to go through his district. When the South seceded, these disagreements became muted as southern routes were ruled out and Republican expansionists came to control Congress.

The transcontinental railroad was a great feat of engineering, ambition, and organization. It also was a source of massive corruption, unnatural concentrations of power, and severe economic pressures that distorted settlers' decisions on where to settle and how to ensure their economic survival. Railroad fixers paid huge bribes to members of Congress and the executive branch, in effect buying huge subsidies—including title to vast tracts of land these private businesses inevitably used to maximize their own profits. Around the same time, homestead acts promised settlers free land for farms and ranches. But the land could be made into viable farms and ranches only if it was linked up through roads that didn't exist, or by the railroads, which determined to control the land they were given for their own purposes. A less unruly people might have accepted the dominion of the railroads, the banks, and their wealthy creatures. Overall, however, western settlers demanded independence and worked to achieve it by hook, crook, and hard work.

Older histories of the West focused on townships' constant cycle of boom and bust. This story had much to be said for it. It reflected common realities and highlighted an important American character trait: the almost instinctive ability to forge communities. Throughout the West, Americans put together, not just buildings, but voluntary organizations (religious, commercial, farmers' and ranchers,' and more informal associations) that fleshed out public life. And they did it with lightning speed. During this era settlers also had to meet new, sometimes difficult requirements to get and keep federal land or, more troubling, federal land granted to railroads with their own agendas. And, if they wanted to survive and thrive, towns often had to work hard to convince railroad companies to include them along their route so that people and commerce would find them. The result was "boosterism"—a combination of town solidarity, celebration, and advertising that many historians mock, but which fostered genuine community spirit and often spurred sustained growth.

Boosters' jobs were made much harder by railroads' arbitrary decisions on where to run their track, and by the unpredictable, alluring, and often destructive offers of free land coming from the federal government. Mistakes were made—often colossal mistakes that cost lives. Perhaps most tragic: the government encouraged homesteaders to settle in areas where long-term farming was simply impossible before the development of mass irrigation systems. But along with these tragedies and many failures came an arc of successful settlement. Homesteaders brought their persistence, entrepreneurial spirit, and a determined ethic of cooperation rooted in the demand that everyone pull his own weight, take care of his own, pitch in with neighbors when circumstances required it and, most important of all, keep his word.

Today we rarely hear about the central role of religion in all this. At the time it was crucial, as it was reflected in books and movies until the recent frontal assault on religion begun a few decades ago. Churches were among the first buildings to go up in any new town. Prayer was a daily practice in families and often in public. Religion, like most other forms of association in the West, was so fundamental that the instinct to support it was deeply ingrained. One thing often missing: actual ministers. Many towns brought their own priest or minister with them. But they were a distinct minority. The towns started up so quickly that finding a minister could be difficult. So, traveling ministers would be wooed to come to town and townspeople became rather accepting of differing (overwhelmingly protestant) forms and attitudes. Townspeople took what they could get or, if they were large enough, joined to vote on what type of minister to bring out from back east. But find a minister they did. And that minister became a central figure, exercising great authority in matters moral and generally public as well as specifically religious.

Bars and brothels were indeed common, especially where large numbers of unattached young men were found—that is, in the larger towns and in the towns where large-scale ranching dominated. But this didn't reflect any extraordinarily loose ideal of virtue. Public morals were of great concern. There was a code—a social contract, the deal for the security and opportunities of living in community in the West—that could be enforced with shunning and even lethal force. Jury nullification and lynching in the South, used to terrorize freedmen, was a corrupt form of long-standing American traditions of public order. Remember the colonists' "riding out of town on a rail" anyone who made himself sufficiently hated? This tradition did not die out early or easily. This form of unruliness, especially where the law seemed distant or insufficient, caused real tragedies—innocents were lynched. But

it shows both the limits of rule of law from above in a nation rooted in customary relations, and the determination of American communities to enforce
rules of conduct the law may not be able to enforce.

A liar, a cheat, a man of no honor, took risk with life and limb as well as
reputation. In *The Long Winter* (one of the *Little House* novels), Laura Ingalls
Wilder told of the severe winter she spent in the Dakota Territory during
1880–1881. Food had become perilously scarce. When the dry goods dealer
sought to profiteer on the situation, the locals got together to threaten him
with violence. The storekeeper then angrily said the customer he had sought
to cheat could take the goods for nothing. The townspeople would not have
that, either. The storekeeper would get the customary price for his goods.

Settler justice could be rough, as it was throughout the West. And the line
between lawman and gunman was often too blurry for the sake of justice.
But rough justice sometimes was the only possible justice, and it was aimed
at maintaining public peace and order in difficult circumstances. With few
lawmen and little statutory law, people often were left to themselves, and
informal rules often had to rule. Even the duel made a comeback as hordes of
unattached young men, determined to make their fortune and name, flooded
the West. The "fair fight" between gunmen, in extreme circumstances at the
edge of law, sometimes had to serve as the means of settling disputes.

In the unsettled West, the federal government set forces in motion it could
not control. It was left to the settlers themselves to organize societies. By way
of example let's consider the Wyoming Stock Growers Association (WSGA),
a frontier organization that shows the range of issues even rather spontaneous
organizations sometimes had to address.

Founded in 1873, just four years after the Wyoming territory itself, the
WSGA was set up as a trade association. Members used it to organize cattle
drives and shipments, keep track of cattle brands, and, most famously, to
fight the often-murderous cattle rustlers who plagued Wyoming. Wyoming
Territory was huge, made up mostly of chunks of territory set aside for
free-range cattle grazing and farm settlement. Problem was, people often
didn't know whether ranchers or farmers had a legal right to water access
or title in many of these areas. Conflicts between farmers and ranchers, and
between small and large ranchers, were inevitable.

The WSGA was accused, rightly in some instances, of abusing its power by
hiring its own detectives and enforcers and siding with its own, larger landholders in disputes with smaller ranchers and farmers. Worst, the WSGA was
the main instigator of the Johnson County War, in which WSGA hired guns
murdered several local farmers and ranchers under cover of fighting rustlers.
The locals formed a posse and a standoff ensued, broken only by the arrival
of US troops.

The trouble had its roots in gangs of cattle rustlers but was made far worse by the general chaos of the time and by the inevitable conflicts between those who wanted to keep their land protected and those who wanted their livestock to roam and graze free. In the Old World such conflicts had arisen centuries before as the rich enclosed common fields for their own use, effectively stripping poorer people of the means to feed themselves. In the American West free land meant that ranchers could dominate the economy and society at the expense of the yeomanry—a situation made far worse because government policy encouraged people to farm areas soon wiped out by drought.

Most surprising was the ability of the WSGA and its adversaries to establish relative peace in Wyoming. Farmers and small ranchers stood up for themselves and were not simply wiped out by their richer, more powerful opponents. The result was neither pretty nor perfectly just. But, as so often in the United States, low-level conflict gave way to a deal, in this case over water and grazing rights. The federal government didn't "solve" the problem until a law passed in 1934. But most local groups came to agreements in their own areas that brought relative peace.

Chapter 14

Rome Wasn't Built in a Day, but Oklahoma City Was

To this day one can hear about Oklahomans re-creating the Land Rush. Children in frontier garb line up on an imaginary border. At the sound of a shot, they rush in to "lay claim" to a patch of earth as their own. Over 130 years ago on these days (there were several) a sprint for new land and the opportunity it brought began with a cannon shot. Anyone who could get to the border of designated former Indian territory near the nation's center could simply run in and stake a claim for free land. The most famous Land Rush began at noon on April 22, 1889. Almost 2 million acres were up for grabs and around fifty thousand people showed up to stake their claim.

Once the cannon was fired on that April day, the would-be settlers rushed, in wagons, on horses, on foot, and stuffed into train cars, to seek the best sites they could. Many simply scouted out good farmland and settled in on these Unassigned Lands (Oklahoma—Choctaw for "red people"—would take some time to become the official name of this and surrounding areas). But about ten thousand people (almost all men at this point, for everyone expected conflict and hardship in the beginning) headed for what would soon become Oklahoma City—a central location near a bend in the river and a watering station for the railroad. By the end of the day all the viable, and much nonviable, land in this area had been claimed by someone, or several competing someones. Tents had sprouted everywhere, along with a few shacks, and township life began.

This explosion of activity did not come out of nowhere, and it was only the beginning of Oklahoma City's story. But it shows both the positive and the negative sides of the American character—as well as the vast, gray area in which self-interest and norms rooted in religion and public spirit had to be sorted out in a way that allowed people to build decent, working townships. The prehistory and development from this single day include a cast of characters and storyline showing the variety of persons and types that continued to make up our settler people.

Settlers "found" towns. There may be a tribe, whether ancient Etruscans in Italy or Cherokee in the United States, up the road. The new settlement may bring amicable trade or murderous conflict. But for a city to grow there first must be a settlement. A specific group of people must decide that a specific piece of land will serve it as a home base. Other people, including individuals, families, communities, and perhaps hostile forces, will add to the new town. But it begins with an act of conscious settlement—though one usually shrouded in mystery and even myth.

In America's early decades, towns were generally founded by tight-knit communities that had formed, on religious and/or ethnic lines, in the Old World. As time went on, it became more common for groups to form in the eastern cities or even on the fly in wagon trains headed west. The old form of community settlement remained powerful. Swedes, freedmen, Germans, and others self-consciously moved to new territories to found towns. But America always had seen another, more chaotic, type of founding. What came to be known as Boomers would simply move into unsettled lands—generally occupied, if loosely, by Indians—and commence hunting, trapping, trading, and farming. Towns often formed around clusters of squatters, sometimes growing into permanent settlements, sometimes being wiped out by Indians, sometimes being driven off by American (or British) soldiers.

As time went on, this less community-based form of settlement became more common. Government rules about who could settle where and how they could gain safe title to their land made it easier and more likely that individuals and smaller groups would chase after land and opportunity on their own. The most extreme case of this type of settlement was Oklahoma City.

Some recent observers have portrayed Oklahoma City's founding as sheer crime and chaos only slowly and imperfectly shaped into a city—mostly by the federal government.[1] Oklahomans prefer a more positive take on their state's origins, one that contemporary libertarians might point to as a kind of spontaneous order growing naturally from individual self-interest. The truth lies somewhere in between, in the low-level conflict naturally produced by an unruly people seeking to forge order and the common good out of conflicting interests and visions.

As with all settlements, Oklahoma's history begins before its founding. Oklahoma grew out of the Indian Territory to which the federal government had consigned Indian tribes who had been dispossessed of their lands, especially the Five Tribes Jackson had forced onto the Trail of Tears. After the Civil War, the federal government stripped an extensive portion of this territory from the Creek and Seminole Indians to whom it had been ceded on the grounds that their members had supported the Confederacy.

Perhaps the first important Oklahoma Boomer was Elias C. Boudinot, a part-Cherokee, one-time Confederate soldier and politician, lawyer, and newspaperman. Boudinot's letter published in the *Chicago Tribune* in 1879 is credited with spawning the Oklahoma Boomer movement by calling for the Indian Territory to be opened to white homesteaders. Boudinot had opened a tobacco business in the territory, then lost it to the government for nonpayment of taxes. Boudinot fought this confiscation all the way to the Supreme Court on the grounds that the taxation violated existing treaties with his tribe. His loss convinced him that Indians had to demand American citizenship and individual land titles that would, in effect, dissolve their tribes in exchange for full legal rights within the United States. He also worked to secure railroad routes through the territory and was accused of choosing his own advancement over the interests of his tribe, though he continued to do business in Indian Territory until his death in 1890.

Boudinot was not, however, the most active booster of white homesteading in what would become Oklahoma. That distinction belongs to William Couch, a publicist who organized several Boomer invasions of Oklahoma well before the land rush. Couch's settlements were always found and disbanded by federal troops who escorted he and his minions, at gunpoint, out of the territory. Eventually, however, Boomer and railroad lobbying secured approval for the Land Rush.

Not long after the cannon fired on April 22, Couch and his supporters were surveying and parceling out what would become Oklahoma City. They were among the first to arrive because they had set up illegal, hidden camps nearby. They proceeded to stake out claims according to their preset plan and sell them to later arrivals. This was flagrantly illegal but many settlers put down money for the closest thing they could find to a guarantee that they would be able to keep the parcel they claimed.

And so, sooners—those who arrived sooner than was legal—took possession of the most valuable land in the area. Other settlers weren't happy and there were threats of violence. But a kind of (lop-sided) compromise was reached. How? It would be convenient to set up a single hero as the anti-Couch, the man of public spirit who took on the tyrants in the name of the people. The most likely candidate for hero, here, would be Angelo Scott.[2] Scott, an educated newspaperman, stepped in almost immediately after Oklahoma City was founded to help negotiate land claims and keep the peace. He also would found Oklahoma City's first newspaper, YMCA, Philharmonic, and First Presbyterian Church. He would eventually be voted "Oklahoma's most useful citizen" and enjoy a long career in education and commerce.

But Scott was far from alone. To begin with, at least two other syndicates had attempted to set out Oklahoma City and their members vigorously

opposed Couch's power. As important, the settlers did not simply sit
back and allow others to lead them. Scott was a crucial organizer of local
self-government but the town meetings were real exercises in local democracy. Men nominated, accepted, and rejected representatives from almost day
one in Oklahoma City. And the committees they formed were selected with
some care. For example, the primary town committee, on which Scott served,
was chosen so that its members would each come from a different state, in
order to foster impartiality. This primary committee was empowered to look
into land claims and lay out a workable city (existing claims left no room for
details like roads, without which there would be gridlock and/or chaos). The
people were no mere mob of followers.

In the short run, at least, Couch got the best of the situation. His certificates
were ratified as valid land claims and his minions, by threatening violence,
managed to keep the syndicate's layout for the center of the city. This meant
losses for more honest settlers and an awkward road layout. Couch even got
himself elected mayor. He resigned after a brief time in power so that he
could capitalize on his own land claim. He was soon dead, shot by a rival
claimant to his plot on the city's outskirts.

There was no need for a founding myth of Oklahoma City. No brothers
suckled by a wolf as with Rome's Romulus and Remus, nor the later fratri-
cide. There was the historical fact of the Land Rush. There also was conflict,
which could have led to much bloodshed, between forces. Good citizens like
Scott kept their heads and (mostly) kept the peace as well. And the scoun-
drels? Many managed to keep dishonest gains. Others died bad deaths. And
the Sooners more generally were domesticated over time. Always happy
to give clever men their due, even if somewhat ruefully, Oklahomans took
the Sooner to their hearts, even making him the mascot of the University
of Oklahoma.

This ambivalence and even affection for the charming trickster and
rule breaker is deeply ingrained in the American character. Cheating in a
face-to-face deal could be bad for your health. But more large-scale trick-
ery was a different matter. Sooners became mascots. P.T. Barnum became a
larger-than-life figure by telling lies (and showing "real" oddities) everyone
knew in their hearts were false. And the gunfighter and lawman became
almost interchangeable in Western lore and popular fiction. Wyatt Earp's
journey from suspected horse thief to lawman was hardly unique; it followed
a pattern that became a central feature in American popular culture. One
example: James Garner's turn in a pair of movies, *Support Your Local Sheriff*
and *Support Your Local Gunfighter* in 1969 and 1971, respectively. Whether
as sheriff or gunfighter, Garner was the smiling con man who used brains
more than brawn (or gun) to bring peace and prosperity to the town, and to
woo the local beauty. Rules were broken, but only on the edges, for the public

good, and with a winning smile. Garner's characters would fight if need be. And they would win, in part at least by bringing the people together to support the rascal who remained a Good Guy.

Americans' local solidarity and the willingness to fight would not always be enough. Westerners would face other great threats to their survival. Especially dangerous were continuing threats from railroads and their backers in banks and the federal government. A specifically western brand of radicalism would arise to fight these combinations. But before we can discuss that radical populism, we first have to discuss the rise of the combinations they faced. For this we now move on to industrial growth in the Northeast.

NOTES

1. See especially Sam Anderson's *Boomtown* (New York: Broadway Books, 2018), a decidedly ambivalent history of Oklahoma that includes all the currently popular disparagement of settlers as thieves and bullies.

2. This is Anderson's story.

Chapter 15

The Pursuit of Consolidation

Historians usually divide post–Civil War America into three regions: North, South, and West. This makes sense because experiences varied widely across these regions. In the South there was dislocation, economic depression, and (usually race-based) violence. Still, people did not merely accept their "fate." Many white yeomen were able to withdraw into their traditional lives of rural self-sufficiency. Many freedmen attempted the same, though with less success, because they were held back (as were their attempts to simply leave the South) by hostile laws, lack of money, and attachment to family and friends who couldn't leave. The old aristocracy, meanwhile, regained much of its former power and used it to avoid duties like paying taxes and, less successfully, to prevent the rise of trade and industry.

Many white yeomen and freedmen had to accept wage labor or agricultural subservience (sharecropping). But they worked hard to build communities. Among former slaves and their children this meant forming associations from burial societies to independent schools. It also meant entering the workforce and maintaining intact, two-parent families at a higher rate than whites into the second half of the twentieth century. Characters and cultures abided even in tough, unjust times.

In the West there was a mad scramble among settlers to seize land and hold it against the efforts of government-subsidized interests, criminals, and displaced Indians. Here also there was violence. But the frontier was open, and it provided opportunity for families to join and forge larger associations that made for a thriving social and economic life. Religion, too, thrived as the people continued to see God calling them to join together in worship, prayer, and decent lives.

In the old Northeast things were no less chaotic. But they brought more sustained change than in the South and more centralized control than in the West. Wars tend to concentrate power. Military discipline and restrictions on private behavior that might interfere with the war effort have to be implemented by some central authority. And once the war is over, the folks who control the levers of power have a hard time letting go. They tend to think there is more good to be done, and that these new powers would make it easier to build bridges, settle territory, and keep the nation united and prosperous. One can almost hear the call: "We won the last war, now we must win the next war"—whether that be a war against the next enemy on the horizon, or against vice, ignorance, or attempts to interfere with the increasing reach of the federal government and those it subsidizes.

It didn't help that states' rights were increasingly identified with slavery and rebellion. Many Americans on both sides of the Civil War thought they were fighting to preserve their local traditions, rights, and ways of life—whether from the federal government or from the power of the slave-owning aristocracy. Now, though, opposing federal intrusion was more and more likely to be taken as disloyalty.

The Republican program of internal improvements, government subsidies for grand public works, and calls for a single, uniform understanding of rights and responsibilities failed utterly in the South. But in the North there was money and political will to make it real. Internal improvements were key. The transcontinental railroad was the most famous of these projects though, while its track was exclusively in the West, its effects were widespread in the North. Bribes were huge, widespread, and catching. The system of buying votes to gain subsidies became commonplace and shaped both national and state policies, especially for railroads, but also for river and road projects. As important, an entirely new class of corporate financiers and lobbyists grew up.

Corporations weren't very common in the pre–Civil War United States. And only companies that were somehow concerned with "the public interest" were given the "corporate" benefits of limited liability and immunity from personal lawsuits. But by the late nineteenth century corporate law itself had been fundamentally transformed. People seeking corporate charters no longer had to bind themselves to a public purpose, or even a particular line of business. Stockholders benefited greatly from reforms. For decades they had been victimized by fraudulent schemes in which their stock was "watered" by predatory managers who sold out and left stock purchasers to pay creditors out of their own pockets. Through limited liability owners of stock gained immunity from personal liability—their stock might become worthless but they could no longer be forced to pay out of their own pockets for the corporation's debts. Unfortunately, such laws also protected dishonest and predatory corporate owners.

The railroads were just one part of America's wider, more powerful industrialization. The trend toward mass production of basic goods like iron and steel, the development of new production techniques requiring large numbers of factory workers, and the financial mechanisms necessary to fund this shift were both inevitable and beneficial to the vast majority of Americans. But it was accomplished at breakneck speed at the cost of empowering the federal government and those men capable of manipulating politicians and their legislation. This corruption directly undermined American traditions of family-centered independence, competition, and a relative balance of power among varied institutions and associations.

Left-wing activists dubbed this the era of "Robber Barons." Others defend barons like David Rockefeller (oil), Cornelius Vanderbilt (shipping), and Andrew Carnegie (steel)—all of whom made vast fortunes thanks in significant part to transportation subsidies and other federal policies. It is true that industrialization made Americans in general more prosperous and economically secure. But many Americans at the time—perhaps especially small business owners—attacked Rockefeller and company as enemies of competition and America's customary standards of decency in economic and social relations. As important, the barons were only the most successful manipulators of new corporate forms. Many more raised funds, sold stock, then bled the corporations dry of funds; they then simply walked away, leaving investors to cover the losses. Markets were rocked repeatedly by bubbles and crashes caused less by market forces than by fraud.

Americans always have been suspicious of large organizations—organizations with which a typical yeoman or family business could not have a "fair fight." Meanwhile, many of the "captains of industry" saw themselves as exactly that: rulers of their ships who should be obeyed, not just by workers, but by anyone seeking to share the seas of commerce with them. This is why Rockefeller felt justified in cutting off his competitors from railroad access—he, like Carnegie and Vanderbilt—saw himself bringing discipline to an "unruly" market under his own control. The competition was not to be beaten in the marketplace but displaced or bought out in ever-larger combinations in the interest of a more "rational" distribution of goods, power, and wealth. The barons prioritized ruthless application of organizational skills and fostered a new class of financiers (J. P. Morgan was the archetype) who sought to reorganize the national economy as a whole.

American workers, accustomed to working for bosses and owners they knew personally, were to be disciplined in the name of efficiency. Resistance was not massive at first, let alone beholden to socialism. American labor unrest through most of the nineteenth century was issue specific. Workers didn't seek "control of the means of production." They fought over working hours (new industries often demanded twelve-hour workdays), wages (often cut during hard times), and conditions (in a time before insurance). Local mayors, police, and even militia often supported their working neighbors during lockouts and strikes. Local authorities supported their own citizens, both small business owners and workers under siege from outsiders' giant economic combinations. Barons hired their own armed enforcers and the federal government increasingly sent federal troops to back them up.

The federal government, supported by the courts, interfered more and more with local police powers. To justify shoving aside local, traditional authority, centralizers in government and the press blamed unrest on radical immigrants. And there were some. But socialism and anarchism were imported plants that failed to take root in America for quite some time. Still, hostility toward immigrants was real and harsh, bringing its own problems. It would backfire in important ways, empowering, not just a general nativism but a reforming elite hostile to traditional American communities.

The concern with mass immigration was not irrational. As in the 1840s, immigrants came in large numbers and included many peasants with differing religions and cultures and without money or many relevant skills. Millions of them were immediately swallowed up, not by rural and small-town life, but by growing industrial cities and hastily, shoddily constructed tenements. Better than the conditions most immigrants left, these slums were shocking to most Americans in their squalor and led to a kind of dependence on local bosses that was hostile to American standards of township-based independence.

The problem was far from universal. In the West immigrants at times founded their own towns, and at times joined the general movement toward independence. In places like rural Ohio even the railroad was part of a kind of natural sorting you can see in smaller villages to this day. New German immigrants, for example, would wait for the conductor to tell them which stops were in Catholic and which in Lutheran towns. Only later, as the towns grew or grew together, would they come to have churches of both types, even as towns of English stock tended to be formed around Methodist churches. Germans (as well as Poles, Yiddish-speaking Jews, and others) maintained their own culture, including newspapers in their own language until Woodrow Wilson, claiming military necessity, forbade the mails from carrying many of them.

Limits on immigration levels would take generations to implement in an era before big government, sparking a renewal of pre–Civil War anti-immigrant sentiments. There were "Blaine Amendments" forbidding public assistance to private, usually Catholic, religious schools (public schools were almost all overtly protestant), and campaigns of "Americanization" unthinkable in earlier eras. Public school lessons in patriotism and national loyalty spread, as did upper-class determination to "civilize" and integrate ethnic groups that, in a more open, rural time, Americans had accepted as separate communities within the American whole. Civil religion—public recitations of national virtues and creeds, that previously had been secondary to expressions of religious faith—now became primary, much to the harm of religion itself.

Evangelical reformers uprooted themselves from local congregations seeking to walk in the ways of their Lord. They increasingly looked to a social gospel demanding social change in the here and now. They became increasingly intent on securing changes in federal policies on issues like temperance, labor, and poverty. These movements were much less successful and widespread than contemporary histories would indicate. American character, and characters, would abide. But a new upper class developed. The courts took on imperial power, striking down state and local laws that sought to protect traditional economic relationships on the grounds that the Constitution dictated a "national market" for all goods and services. Meanwhile, regular Americans rejected a growing, more centralized national power structure. The stage was set for a populist revolt and the strange rise of progressivism, an American movement dedicated to America's fundamental transformation.

Chapter 16

Wall Street vs. Main Street

The Early Years. Or, from
Populism to Progressivism

Americans were on the move during the late nineteenth century. They were settling the West and building an industrial economy, especially in the Northeast and Midwest. With their strong entrepreneurial spirit and work ethic Americans produced new inventions and companies. But over all this hung the shadow of giant combinations spawned and supported by the federal government. These combinations threatened to strangle the livelihoods of small business owners, their workers and, most noticeably, farmers and ranchers. Westerners had been urged to settle the frontier quickly and had done so. But thanks in large measure to misguided federal policies, their settlements were cut off from any naturally growing system of roads and rivers and their farms and ranches had to be large—too large for subsistence farming to work. And so, to survive and flourish, Westerners were forced to rely on a very few railroads and the few wholesale dealers (granaries and livestock shippers) connected with them. Rural Southerners suffered from many of the same maladies but because their governments were so poor and their public life so riven by violence, they would play a lesser role in the political drama to come.

Westerners found themselves at the mercy of federally subsidized power brokers and they didn't like it. Self-sufficiency of the old type was all but impossible in the dry, as-yet un-irrigated West so they had to deal with monopolies and near-monopolies based thousands of miles away. Add to this the power of banks to foreclose on farms and ranches with little notice and you have a recipe for real financial oppression and, in America, near rebellion.

The resulting political movement—populism—was at times quite radical in its political program. Populist leaders ended up rejecting the efforts of a strong-willed group of "anti-monopolists" who worked directly and specifically to break up railroads and their enablers. Buying into the increasingly (and sadly) common view at the time that massive organizations were inevitable, populists demanded government ownership of railroads and banks. Their argument: if their livelihoods were to depend on monopoly power, that power should at least be liable to democratic control. This option smacked of socialism and therefore was doomed in an America not yet sufficiently degraded to embrace government control over basic elements of economic life. But populism itself was not a socialist movement. There was no dream of a "workers' paradise" or of material equality. Opportunity was the watchword; opportunity playing out in traditional, local communities, natural associations, and especially a way of life rooted in family farm and ranch.

Populist organizations had some local victories and eventually fielded a presidential candidate (William Jennings Bryan) who captured the Democratic nomination, though not the presidency. But Populism failed to break up the monopolies besieging rural America and eventually was swallowed by a countermovement, progressivism. That movement promised help for small businesses but produced America's first administrative state—a beast in its very nature devoted to empowering bureaucrats within a single nation of concentrated powers.

Unlike rural, tradition-based populism, progressivism was deeply ingrained in urban, upper-middle class structures and values. The drive for "clean government" helped launch the movement as an attack on big-city political machines. But anti-corruption was only a small part of the progressive program. Where small-town, Main Street reformers sought to simply clean up local politics, progressives formed a national movement aimed at transforming American government. Their leaders, including Presidents Theodore Roosevelt (TR) and Woodrow Wilson, did not really share populists' concern with monopoly power. No enemies to Wall Street, progressives sought to control monopolies at the federal level rather than uproot them.

Progressives worked to nationalize reform. As we've discussed, Americans early on developed a certain drive for perfectionism and a habit of combining with their neighbors to improve people's character as well as their physical environment. But things changed during the late nineteenth century, especially for the self-anointed "respectable" leaders concerned to inculcate new, more uniform, national standards of good character.

In part the progressive concern with order in the United States was understandable. Americans' relationship with law and order has always been a bit ambiguous. We don't line up quite as well for planes, trains, and buses as the British. But we insist that line-jumpers be kicked out of our amusement parks. Claim jumpers in the gold fields might get away with it, but they also might be shot or lynched. And we rebelled against our British overlords by appealing to a higher law—not some vague set of principles or "conscience," but a deeper, ingrained law from Magna Carta, colonial charters, and, underlying them all, a natural law we understood applies to every person and people.

Americans ordered their lives, not through slavish obedience to written rules or established rulers, but on the grounds of respect for general norms and the need for order within changing circumstances. All this meant that the American character, a set of habits rooted in shared culture, was never automatically, instantaneously transferred to new arrivals. And there had been millions of new arrivals over the course of the mid to late nineteenth century.

Some of the new arrivals did not plan to stay—not just Asians (especially Chinese people brought over in large numbers under limited work contracts) but various European immigrants sought to make some money then return home. But more stayed and, while their very willingness to leave home for a foreign land showed the same adventuring spirit deep within the American character, they brought with them customs and attitudes from their homelands as well. And, as we noted earlier, many were unable to either assimilate by immediately submerging themselves in American communities or, more commonly, take their communities with them to areas where they could form more local ties and specifically American social habits over time. Rather, the concentration of power, population, and jobs in the inner cities, multiplied manyfold by federal policies, caused them to huddle in urban tenements, forming something unheard of in America—a nascent "working class" seeking, not to climb the ladder of economic success, but to secure a more comfortable life where they already were.

This was far from the only fate of later immigrants. The dream of self-governance remained widespread; shops and small businesses founded by immigrants continued to flourish. Entire towns in the West were formed by communities from Ireland, Germany, and Scandinavia, for example. But there were enough poor, uneducated immigrants to shape an urban landscape that caused panic among native-born elites.

Americans had always been a *dis*-organized people. We were happy to form a variety of associations but unlikely to form lasting national organizations. Even political parties were coalitions of more local groups rather than uniform ideological movements. We were too centered on where we lived to think in national political terms, although we were comfortable with broader notions of a common people with a destiny of local self-government. But the sheer size of urban slums and machines, like the size of corporate trusts, spawned fear and dangerously "big" thinking. The result: a new reformism that owed less to local communities than to a vision of a truly united nation sharing, not just general characteristics, but a single, common culture. The local reforms Americans had pursued for decades by the late nineteenth century took on a more radical and certainly more centralizing character. The results, generally lauded today, were not positive for American townships and character.

There is no better example of how the nationalization of reform could bring disaster than the temperance movement. Concern about public drunkenness and alcoholism's tendency to undermine individual and especially family life went back at least to the antebellum era. Temperance began as a movement among voluntary associations. Members were called on to pledge, not abstinence, but *temperance*, that is self-restraint. Hard-drinking settlers and respectable shopkeepers pledged in front of friends and neighbors to drink only in moderation. Over time, and especially in certain isolated areas, local ordinances restricted and even prohibited publicly serving (and drinking) alcohol. But it was only at the end of the nineteenth century that a movement began to ban alcoholic beverages altogether as an ungodly drain on public virtue and family funds. Anti-saloon leagues of various sorts fomented occasional acts of violence but more often pushed for legislation. The Woman's Christian Temperance Union was among the most powerful of these groups. Its best-known leader, Frances Willard, was a noted feminist who emphasized the WCTU's interest in women's suffrage and a variety of public health and reform measures associated with Christian socialism.

Eventually groups like the WCTU succeeded in imposing national Prohibition through a constitutional amendment. That amendment fostered the growth of organized crime and failed utterly in its purpose. It also served as the greatest triumph of an ideology of public morals that substituted national laws for local social action.

The WCTU, Anti-Saloon League, and other prohibition groups were just part of a broader movement for social reform. Often led by protestant ministers, these groups aimed to "clean up" the public square and teach immigrants and poor people to be "good Americans." They picked up on earlier attempts to make the public schools into shapers of national citizenship. They also supported "settlement houses" where upper-class people would live among the poor in order to show them how to act. Men and women in these organizations believed they were bringing God's plan to fruition in this world by reforming society and human character. The more clearly dark side of this reform was that form of social or moral hygiene we call eugenics. Reformers, doctors, and judges supported sterilization programs for the mentally "unfit," and birth control and abortion programs aimed especially at African Americans. Mixing bad science with earthly religion, they believed those beneath them in wealth, station, and morals should be uplifted or eliminated through national programs. Americans would be shaped into the highly idealized and uniform "100 percent Americans" TR vigorously demanded in his attacks on German Americans in particular.

Progressivism built on this reformism, promising a better, more scientific, and more virtuous nation. It gained bipartisan appeal because it promised swift, effective action to organize American society, controlling rather than abolishing new concentrations of power. Wilson, the leading intellectual of progressivism, began in the late nineteenth century to propose sweeping changes in our constitutional structure to end the "deadlock of democracy." Rejecting the framers' insistence that only limited, separated powers could be trusted as the tools of a free people, Wilson (like TR) proposed an empowered presidency and various items of more direct democracy to put the will of the people into effect quickly and efficiently. As important, a new, professional class of administrators would run federal agencies to ensure the safety and well-being of the people. Food, drugs, working conditions, the money supply, the economy's proper functioning, all would be entrusted to experts above and beyond politics.

Slowly at first, progressives began building an administrative state. They promised to make real the will of the people by turning abstract laws demanding good ends like fair trading practices and safe working conditions into specific rules that would govern powerful actors. They soon established a governing elite beyond the people's control.

Administrative growth started slowly, with agencies like the Interstate Commerce Commission (formed in 1887) intended to prevent the railroads from colluding unfairly against their customers. Attempting to ride herd on the leviathan it had created, the federal government at least wrote a recognizable law with clear standards to be enforced by the commissioners. And the federal government followed up with the Sherman Antitrust Act in 1890, intended to prevent trusts that ran railroads and other enterprises from entering into agreements not to compete with one another (in other words maintaining their monopoly power) and otherwise control entire markets. Unfortunately, this law was misinterpreted by courts to apply, in practice, only to labor unions—said to be "restricting trade" by forming combinations to compete with the power of the corporations. Thus, courts undermined the purposes of both relevant acts, preventing the breakup of the trusts, but also preventing local workers from defending themselves against national trusts.

American courts were both more honest and more highly respected than most throughout the world. Unfortunately, this gave them a rather elevated sense of their own wisdom and importance, especially at the federal level where they were immune to public recall. This arrogance has brought real problems for our society. When our judges have lost track of their fundamental duty to uphold the law of the land—the preexisting rules rather than their own opinions of how things ought to be—we all have paid a heavy price.

After the Civil War, the Supreme Court rejected the pleas of freedmen in particular to find in the Fourteenth Amendment a reason to protect them from hostile forces. Other groups also had called on the court to protect them from state actions in the early years. But the Justices rightly rejected the kind of decision it had handed down in *Dred Scott*, in which it went beyond the law as traditionally understood to impose an abstract understanding of "the rights of property" (and the hatred of one race). Instead, judges stuck to a traditional understanding of the very real limits of federal power: Congress might make specific laws to enforce all Americans' rights to life, liberty, and property. But only state actions violating these rights could be forbidden and it was up to the states themselves to control their own people's actions in keeping with their always-retained police powers.

This changed by the end of the nineteenth century. A new set of justices began asserting that the rights of property, and especially the freedom of contract, are absolute—that they owe nothing to common-law understandings of morality or local police powers. This "laissez faire" court dominated political as well as economic life for more than a generation. In a series of decisions over the next few decades this court made it impossible for states and localities to bring the trusts under control and, more generally, to exercise their traditional police powers to serve the common good, for example, by keeping young children out of factory work.

Courts struck down laws and actions that might prevent a property owner from getting maximum value on the market for his land, equipment, or investment capital. Labor actions and local regulations of all kinds were declared unlawful because they impinged on the right to contract. Ironically, even as the court claimed to be protecting the businesses' contract rights they upheld state "Jim Crow" laws forcing various businesses to segregate whites from blacks, including in trains, hotels, and other public accommodations historically liable to federal rules. The court noticed no contradiction.

National politics had devolved into a conflict between Wall Street financial interests demanding low wages and increased concentrations of power to maximize industrial efficiency, and Main Street defenders of traditional rural and small-town life, who sought to keep industrial organizations woven into local communities. Immigration and "hard money" kept wages low and prices high. Eventually Main Street made some progress in limiting immigration (sometimes on explicitly racial grounds, more often as a means of maintaining the preexisting character of Americans and their society), though very little in reducing federal policies maintaining high prices.

Progressivism promised rule by the people, guided by the denizens of a different, future street—what might be named "Agency Street"—the home of federal bureaucrats. The claim was that politics in America were ruled by money men and their servants, along with older aristocracies in states and localities. The answer, progressives declared, was more direct rule by the will of the people as interpreted and implemented by experts insulated from the public.

World War I further empowered the federal government. There had been great opposition to entering the war on the grounds that it wasn't America's fight. Wilson, who had openly sided with Britain and France from the beginning, insisted that Germany was violating America's rights as a neutral nation. Eventually a combination of German actions and the administration's (and the press's) reactions brought a declaration of war. Wilson understandably exercised the powers of his office to win that war. He also used them to seek out and crush suspected disloyalty and press demands for public displays of national loyalty.

Like the Civil War, World War I increased the size of government. The following two administrations worked hard to reduce the size and impact of that government. Ultimately, they failed, and left in place the essential elements of economic regulation that would bring, and capitalize on, a Great Depression. The stage was set for open conflict, not between the usual small-scale associations and institutions that always had been at odds in American history, but increasingly among large, powerful institutions—multistate corporations, the federal government, and national unions.

Americans had gone through a time of great transformation. From a federal constitutional republic, progressives had sought to turn the United States into a democratic nation—one nation, indivisible—administered by a new class of politically neutral experts. Tocqueville had observed that American liberty was not merely dependent upon, but in its essence woven into administrative decentralization. Americans always had ruled themselves through custom as much as law, through association as much as political structure. In the frontier West and the "backward" South, this remained the case, by and large. But in the Northeast and the old Midwest this increasingly was no longer true. The balance had now been tipped toward more formal means of social control, based now in Washington DC. As Robert Nisbet would later observe, communities survive only when they have a purpose. American communities always had had deep purpose for Americans—the people organized their lives through local associations—including but by no means dominated by local political associations. Time would tell how well they would respond to the crises to come within communities with less purpose.

Immediate results were mixed. African Americans undoubtedly saw a degradation of their rights. Segregation was formalized and extended, enforced now by formal laws as well as less formal violence, even lynching. Wilson had even extended segregation, not only banishing African Americans from the White House staff but segregating a federal civil service that had served as a source of dignity and upward mobility to them for decades.

Women, on the other hand, extended their activities and formal rights, cul-minating in passage of a constitutional amendment granting them a national right to vote. Women's public role had been extended throughout this period as they played significant roles, not only in the suffrage movement, but in the Anti-Saloon League and the Settlement Movement. Elizabeth Cady Stanton, Francis Willard, and Jane Addams were leaders in these movements seeking a more uniform set of upstanding characters in national life. And Margaret Sanger, founder of Planned Parenthood, agitated tirelessly for eugenics and birth control, including as a means to reduce what she saw as the menace of African American procreation.

A national administration. Nationalized concerns over culture and morality. National corporations and labor unions. America had been bound together more tightly than ever before by a network of institutions, associations, and political issues. Yet most Americans still lived in their families and local associations, looking to their neighbors rather than officials in Washington for the elements of a decent life. Attention would now be on the center, but the periphery would survive. The question was whether its many elements retained the power to shape and protect the character of an unruly people in times of increased, centralized regimentation.

Chapter 17

A Generation of Change

After World War I there was a "return to normalcy," as President Warren G. Harding put it. Troops were sent home, the military establishment was largely dismantled, and much of the machinery of military discipline, including Wilson's internal oversight of citizens, rationing, and wage and price controls was ended. The economy boomed.

Historians focus on the innovations in this economy: Wall Street played a far larger role than ever before; stock traders had gained power and influence over the last century; and the corporate combinations of the pre–World War I era had come out of the war stronger than ever, joined by war-related industries and new manufacturers. More, an increasingly urbanized population, many of its members now exposed to military regimentation for the first time, were more open than before to the life of Big Commerce. Big Credit was a substantial part of the mix, with trading "on margin" normalized as people and banks incurred massive debt in order to capitalize on the expanding economy.

But, while a substantial number of American adventurous spirits were now focused on stock speculation, this was far from all Americans. Most Americans worked hard to go back to their accustomed lives on farms, ranches, and Main Street. Unfortunately, the Wall Street bubble was real, would have serious consequences, and would serve as another overstated example to justify federal regulation.

Conservative President Calvin Coolidge pointed Americans to their traditional values and associations as he fought to shrink the size of government. Then, in 1928, he retired and handed the reins of power over to a progressive from his own (Republican) party. Coolidge had derisively dubbed Herbert Hoover "Wonder Boy" on account of his fondness for great projects of organization and social engineering. Hoover was convinced that he could avoid what he conceived of as the twin dangers of unregulated commerce and socialism; he would use the federal government as an organizing tool, maintaining the primacy of private capital while maximizing efficiency and

137

lessening the effects of the persistent booms and busts of the industrial business cycle.

Unfortunately for the nation (and the world), only months after Hoover became president the stock market crashed. The Wall Street bubble burst, and the fallout was severe. People and banks went bankrupt. But the ensuing recession only became the Great Depression when credit dried up completely. And this happened only after the much-vaunted Federal Reserve Board—a progressive innovation intended to prevent bank failures by supporting these institutions during panics—acted on its progressive principles. Federal Reserve Chairman (and banking baron) Andrew Mellon insisted that small banks be allowed to fail, that they be "weeded out" so that the large banks might regularize (i.e. concentrate power within) the banking system. The result was a catastrophic shrinking of the money supply—drying up investment funds and bringing a cascade of foreclosures and failures.

In the past, Americans had endured economic downturns by turning to local associations and charities, by organizing relief efforts within their communities, and sometimes by seeking help from their state governments. Hoover would not stand by as his predecessors had and let the economy recover. Progressive that he was, he vastly expanded the federal government's role in the economy. He increased federal spending, provided huge subsidies to farmers (encouraging overproduction) then paid farmers not to plant, pressured businesses to maintain wage rates at a time of falling prices and massive unemployment, and imposed huge tax hikes. Often blamed for not doing enough, Hoover engaged in the same kinds of economic planning Franklin Roosevelt would try years later, to equally disastrous effect. What Hoover failed to do was offer the kinds of symbolic aid that traditionally had quieted people's fears and assured them that their suffering mattered to the people as a whole.

During previous depressions the federal government, recognizing the limits of its legitimate power, had limited its actions to increasing public works where it could and putting money in some people's hands by giving bonuses to veterans. Wonder Boy rejected such old-fashioned salves to public wounds. Years earlier, World War I veterans had been given bonus money certificates (pensions weren't yet administratively possible) that were not payable until 1948. In 1932 an unarmed, peaceful, and respectful Bonus Army of veterans came to Washington seeking early payment on the certificates. Hoover ordered that the marchers be dispersed and evicted, with their wives and children, from their campsite. Hundreds were injured and two veterans died in the resulting violence.

Hoover would be thrown ignominiously from office, to be replaced by a man of few thoughts and no principles, but who would encourage the people to look to Washington as their protector in tough times. Franklin Roosevelt

(FDR) went beyond early progressivism in the name of a New Deal in which the well-being of the people would be guaranteed, not by their own efforts, families, and communities, but by a national state.

Accepting the Democratic nomination for President in 1932, FDR declared he would "break foolish traditions." Invoking Woodrow Wilson, he pledged to "resume the country's interrupted march along the path of real progress, of real justice, of real equality for all of our citizens, great and small."[1] He proposed in this speech a "new deal" for the American people in which the federal government would provide work and security. He would provide neither in practice but would use methods reminiscent of Wilson's wartime mobilization to establish an administrative state devoted to guaranteeing economic security for all. That guarantee would never be (and could never be) performed in a free society, but it would shape American politics ever after.

During the first one hundred days of his administration, FDR established a host of new agencies and programs aimed at providing work and security. Several programs expanded traditional public works. Others doled out federal money to favored states and localities for public relief and aimed to prop up the banking system. The latter instituted new federal regulations aimed at undoing the damage done by previous federal regulations while adding guarantees for depositors' security.

The most far-reaching program of "the First New Deal" was the National Recovery Administration. This agency was set up to deal with the supposed problem of excessive competition in the American economy. Dismissing the very idea of antitrust legislation and putting his faith in the power of government planning, FDR decreed cooperation between the federal government and large corporations to enact a set of codes for "fair" wages, prices, and working conditions and increasing the power of unions. In effect, cartels—small groups of large businesses within each industry—were empowered to write detailed, onerous and often unenforceable codes (some had the actual force of law) that squeezed out smaller businesses, bankrupting them and destroying their workers' jobs.

Hundreds of suits were brought against small businesses for violating NRA codes. One of these suits, *A.L.A. Shecter Poultry Corp. v. U.S.*[2] made its way to the Supreme Court; a unanimous court held that the legislation that decreed formation of the NRA (the "National Industrial Recovery Act") was unconstitutional. For decades, the court had been enforcing a definition of contract rights not in the Constitution. But it had never stopped demanding that the people be ruled by law. The heart of America's primary deal was the rule of law. And the rule of law required that all laws be truly law—most importantly that all federal statutes meet the requirements of the federal constitution. That constitution allows only Congress to write legislation. Only Congress—not a presidential agency, let alone a cartel of corporations—is authorized to write codes of conduct one can be prosecuted for violating. With its NRA enabling legislation, Congress had abdicated to the president the power to legislate; a power he in turn had delegated to favored private parties. The court saw the danger this posed to Americans' self-government.

Unfortunately, *Schechter* marked the last time the court would strike down federal legislation because the law was effectively written by bureaucrats instead of the people's representatives in Congress. And, even as the First New Deal failed to produce the promised return to work and security, a new wave of programs were set to solidify a national administrative state. A Second New Deal was instituted in 1935–1936. It included more works programs, but also a punitive new tax law (the top rate on income was 79 percent) aimed at redistributing income, along with legislation favoring large unions and a Social Security Act that institutionalized federal welfare programs that are with us to this day. It established a permanent system of universal retirement pensions (Social Security), unemployment insurance, and welfare benefits for handicapped and needy children in families without a father present. Social Security would be expanded several times and end up altering fundamentally American culture by shifting old age security from a family to a national government concern.

Please don't misunderstand us. We are not calling for some doomed, unkind, and ultimately misguided crusade to eliminate Social Security. This decades-old program has become essential to the financial survival of tens of millions of Americans who have paid into a system they were told would provide for them in their old age. But it's important to note how and why the program was started as well as its effects on American society. The program began as a simple insurance scheme like those that already existed in some states. People would pay in, the money would be invested, and they would receive payments according to how much they paid in as retirement income.

Even at its start, Social Security was part of a wider program of unemployment and disability benefits that pushed aside state, local, and nongovernmental efforts. Soon after Social Security became law it was expanded to include funds taken from the general treasury (or public borrowing) so that people who had paid in little or nothing would still receive minimum payments. In succeeding decades, the program would take on responsibilities for health care and otherwise expand far beyond any rational self-paid insurance scheme. It became a national program of financial security for all. At each step this federal program nationalized and turned into legal requirements what had been family and local duties to care for the sick, the aged, and the infirm. People had fallen through the cracks of this informal system, just as today they fall through the cracks of a much more extensive, intrusive bureaucratic system. Our point is merely that these programs took away one more reason for the family, the local association, and the local public square, to exist. They further diverted Americans' attention from those around them to political structures in Washington. This regimentation of social security would have a deep impact on the American character.

FDR's New Deal would prolong the Depression for years by stifling job growth, innovation, and investment. By 1939 official unemployment remained over 17 percent and New Dealers were proclaiming economic stagnation the new normal. Only World War II would lift America out of depression. But FDR took the opportunity to change the very nature of government in the United States and with it make a real change in the character of the American people. And he would be popular during and long after his presidency, for that presidency would be judged, not on its ability to create jobs and financial security (it failed at both) but to produce "hope" and change. By subjecting increasingly desperate people to a maelstrom of contradictory policies, he insured that they would look ever more desperately to the federal government for safety and security.

In 1938, despite his failures, FDR ran and won an unprecedented third term. He even ran and won another term four years later, when he knew of the illness that would take his life soon after taking office, making him our only president for life. His real impact: causing the people to look to the federal government to guarantee that they would enjoy the basic elements of a decent life. That "decent life" was in the eye of the beholder; its elements were a matter of (elite) opinion and would change over time. So, too, would the elements of constitutional law and traditions that had, until this time, limited the terms and powers of political office.

NOTES

1. Franklin Delano Roosevelt, "Address Accepting the Presidential Nomination at the Democratic National Convention in Chicago," *The American Presidency Project,* July 2, 1932, accessed June 9, 2022, https://www.presidency.ucsb.edu/documents /address-accepting-the-presidential-nomination-the-democratic-national-convention -chicago-1.

2. 295 U.S. 495 (1935).

Chapter 18

A Changed Generation

Postwar America is closer to us in time but seems further in public imagination than even colonial America because we are so flooded with images of it—images that are distorted by contempt. Hollywood's hatred for 1950s America is deep and merciless. Movies and television portray a sexually repressed, religiously obsessed, and judgmental culture in which women are trapped in sterile suburbs and men spend their lives traveling the roads to offices where they sexually harass their secretaries, get drunk, and cheat the workingman. Even these privileged men had real problems. Conformity ruled in dress, behavior, and opinion in a world where imaginary Communists lurked under every bed and everyone who counted worked feverishly to keep African Americans in the role of invisible servants and everyone vied to be the biggest patriot on the block.

Of course, the caricature says more about Hollywood than the America of this era. The contempt for family, faith, and local freedoms is palpable. What's more, Americans during this era were not so different from Americans from previous times (not that that would lessen Hollywood's contempt). Whatever their race, they continued to get and stay married, to work hard and strive to better themselves as they raised kids within communities of worship and local civic pride.

Americans during the 1950s continued to be what they had been for all our existence: members of families and a variety of associations who worked hard to improve their economic well-being and to improve their neighborhoods and communities. In 1950 a third of Americans still lived in rural areas, even as many city dwellers sought the open spaces and independence of home ownership offered in expanding suburbs. The consumer explosion of the era was real. It raised standards of living. It was expressive and joyous. What is a fin on a car but an expression of sheer joy in the act of movement? There was a very real race problem, which we'll address in the next chapter. For now we note that African Americans were no mere victims; they worked hard to organize and press for civil rights. As to Communism, since the end of the

Cold War and the opening of various Soviet files we have learned, beyond doubt, that there were hundreds of spies working for the federal government, that the Soviets did have a plan in place for offensive, potentially nuclear war, that, in short, Americans had reason to be worried, though not to give up their essential liberties.

Still, hard experience had wrought changes on America and Americans. The dislocations and deprivations of the Great Depression ended only with the beginnings of World War II. Millions died in that war, and those who survived were marked forever by the experience of mass mobilization and regimentation. To a much greater degree than after the relatively brief World War I, the fallout from World War II was a massive and apparently permanent centralization of the economy as well as government.

The men and women who came home from the battlefields and the factories had endured much thanks to their strong spirit. But they also had been disciplined. They had not just suffered but also gotten used to working in gargantuan hierarchical organizations. Unlike the generations before them, many of these Americans had become accustomed to answering to higher authorities, subordinating their own judgement to that of others, not just for some specific good or limited time, but as a matter of habit, for the sake of long-term goals and security. The federal government would not retain such total control over their lives. But Americans of this era trusted the government they identified with escape from depression and war as no other generation had done, and other large organizations, especially big Business and big Labor, would take on a larger role than ever before. In each case the role was guaranteed by a still-powerful federal state that settled into its new role as guarantor of the public good.

America emerged from the war as the most powerful nation on earth. For a brief time, before the full scale of the Soviet threat became openly recognized, Americans thought they could return to normalcy once again, more prosperous than ever before. The federal government was determined to avoid the dislocations normally attending demobilization by enacting massive benefits programs like the G.I. Bill, which sent millions of veterans to college, and federal mortgage subsidies. The crushing taxation of the depression and war era continued to supply money for these expanded programs.

There would be no return to pre-Depression America. Harry Truman tried to expand FDR's New Deal with a "Square Deal," bringing socialized medical care and more. A Republican Congress prevented the massive expansion Truman wanted but failed to roll back FDR's legacy. Another brief war, this time dubbed a "police action" and aimed at showing Western solidarity in the face of Chinese and other Communist aggression on the Korean peninsula, reiterated wartime discipline as the Cold War began. And America took on

the role of world policeman, shouldering the expenses and cultural dislocations it brought.

People's lives were made better by cheaper methods of producing houses,
cars, and other consumer goods—not to mention tariffs and an infrastructure
unscathed by World War II. That said, the comforts of suburbia were pur-
chased at the cost of independence and variety. They were not, in fact, produced by a thriving free market, but by a small number of corporations that
owed their profits to federal programs and regulations that stifled attempts
to form and grow smaller firms. As several times before, a natural flow of
American entrepreneurial spirit was directed and diluted by centralizing programs. Americans sought freedom as well as comfort in the suburbs but, by
buying prepackaged goods subsidized by the government, they brought taxes
and regulations with them that they had never experienced before.

Then came Eisenhower. In 1952, after passage of a constitutional amendment to prevent any Truman repeat of FDR's lifetime presidency, Americans
replaced him with the war hero Dwight D. "Ike" Eisenhower, a moderate
who accepted the New Deal's central programs as part of America's political
landscape. His administration seemed so passive in a time of great crises that
some on the right openly wondered if he might be a Communist. Conservative
writer Russell Kirk had the best response: "Ike isn't a Communist, he's
a golfer."

Kirk was a key figure in the development of a new, self-consciously conservative movement. He and his allies sought to counteract the bad effects
of administrative centralization and of managerial and academic elites who
were increasingly hostile to traditional American values, especially religion.
This was a tall order at a time when mainstream Protestantism in particular
had fallen under the spell of the social gospel, reducing many churches to
local community centers with occasional emissions of bad music. Traditional
conservatives like Kirk, devoted to preserving American culture and politics as formed by Biblical religion and habits, found themselves allied, in
particular through the person and magazine (*National Review*) of William
F. Buckley, with two other significant forces. "Libertarians" propounded an
ideology of individual autonomy in the face of all social and political forces;
they remained in the coalition for decades on account of the common enemy
represented by an increasingly intrusive federal government. Cold Warriors
of various (often basically socialist) stripes also found a home in this movement; they allied with Buckley largely because of the massive blowback
from Joseph McCarthy's bungled anti-communist activities. McCarthy's
ham-fisted tactics empowered leftist journalists and academics and undermined elite support for strong defensive action in the face of the Soviet threat.
Traditionalists often found themselves marginalized by both these narrow
groups; their commitment to American traditions of local self-government

and avoidance of unnecessary foreign entanglements were in keeping with the habits of most Americans but never commanded majority support within their strange "fusionist" coalition.

Quiet "normalcy" reigned in Washington. But the new normal included what Ike himself warned was becoming a "military-industrial complex." This complex was not some fascist plot, but a distinctly middle-of-the-road establishment. Businesses dependent on federal contracts cooperated with military officials (as well as university officials looking for government grants), not to undermine American safety, but to reconfigure spending priorities to align with their own interests. It was not treason, but somewhat blind and smug self-interest in keeping with the psychology of all insiders within power structures, even in free governments.

Progressivism was becoming ever more entrenched as the federal government took ever more responsibility for providing Americans' "guns and butter." The price was a certain conformity. More and more men worked within corporate structures or byzantine union rules and hierarchies. Wages rose (until competitor nations recovered from the war) but work was more regimented than ever. More women than ever were raising their children in rising prosperity and running their communities' churches, libraries, and voluntary associations. But unease and boredom grew with a bland, mass-produced culture, especially among young people who had not experienced the deprivations that made normalcy such a relief for so many.

And one more massive change almost by chance transformed the American cultural landscape. The freeway system began as an Eisenhower defense measure to facilitate movement of troops and matériel. Congress expanded it into a network linking all the major and even minor cities. Car culture exploded as Americans took to the open, four-lane road. The rebel in the fast car became an American icon, even if the only law broken was the speed limit.

Ironically, even as the freeways brought Americans closer to one another in travel time, they pushed them apart. Massive subsidies for new public works crippled what remained of the last grand public works—railroads. The federal government laid down vast ribbons of concrete, not just in the open prairies, but in cities and towns, and on the corpses of neighborhoods in the way of "progress." Suburbs were a relief, but for the young they were also rather boring because their builders neglected to include actual towns with public spaces where people could gather for worship, entertainment, and civic life. A richer but more passive generation watched its children sour on their way of life.

Chapter 19

Civil Rights and the Antidiscrimination State

America has never been placid, even in the "normal" 1950s. Conflicts over the Cold War were real, as were ethnic divisions (especially in the major cities). And there was racism. The South had especially serious issues on this score on account of pervasive policies of segregation (though segregation existed in some form in many non-Southern states as well). The assaults on dignity—relegation to the back of the bus, laws barring entry to most hotels, restaurants, and main sections of entertainment venues—were clear, as was biased use of literacy tests to deny African Americans the vote. Anyone who stepped out of line was liable to arrest, beating, and even lynching.

The South had been left out of much of the economic boom of the postwar era. The Republican Party had given up on the region at the end of Reconstruction. Southern white elites were taken back into the Democratic Party establishment on the basis of their own separate "Deal": national Democrats would not threaten Jim Crow so long as white leadership stayed loyal to the national party and accepted a smaller share of federal projects. This allowed great freedom in some rural areas, where subsistence farming, community life, and local folkways could still rule. It also allowed for great injustice.

African Americans faced a regime that denied them rights of citizenship. Even the basic right to exit was at times contested. Early in the century Henry Ford had to send his own enforcers to protect African Americans determined to leave debt bondage for decent-paying jobs in Detroit. Defenders of the South are right to object that such a partial picture of life in its traditional, family centered, religious, and largely rural communities is harsh and unfair. But we are here focusing on a specific, harsh reality.

African Americans who returned from military service were not looking for a return to the "normalcy" of segregation. FDR had done nothing for them (they were almost all Republicans in any event). But after having fought and

147

seen friends die fighting for the nation, there was a palpable feeling that full citizenship was owed those who risked and often paid the ultimate price. Those who served in Korea had done so in integrated units, making the return to segregation even more galling. White soldiers also had served in integrated units, experiencing the full humanity of African Americans. And people living in nonsegregated parts of the country could more easily travel to, and see on television, segregated areas, and morally objectionable events there. As the civil rights movement gained steam in the 1950s its leaders were able to engage a wider audience and gain broader support among whites who, because of Jim Crow, were the ones with almost all the votes.

After the Civil War, when Congress failed to pass, implement, and enforce legislation guaranteeing basic due process rights to African Americans, Reconstruction failed. Now Congress had another chance, and far more administrative capacity, to force state authorities to protect African Americans from biased court rules, racially charged juries, and hostile state and local officials. But segregationist states held outsized power in Congress and refused to support legislation aimed at securing civil rights for all. Members of Congress not beholden to race-based hierarchies lacked sufficient will and influence to pass laws protecting African American rights.

Many in the South and elsewhere would object to any national intervention in local affairs. And it's important to recognize that not all of this opposition was based in racial animus. Some opposed giving the federal government yet more power, others simply wanted social peace. But the changes wrought by the previous two decades made the status quo as untenable as it was unjust. The question was how much violence would accompany change, and whether that change would bring African Americans fully into the American way of life, or instead change that way of life.

Most civil rights stories at this stage focus on *Brown v. Board of Education*,[1] the Supreme Court decision declaring that segregated public schools are inherently unequal, hence unconstitutional. The *Brown* court was clearly correct in recognizing segregation's immorality and damage to human dignity. Unfortunately, its judicial approach owed too much to previous, bad precedents and so failed to empower African Americans to enter full citizenship.

Beginning with *Dred Scott* (if not before) the court had been taking power to itself to declare various "fundamental rights" (like that to property in slaves) that undermined our constitutional structures and our ability as a people to work toward the common good. The court in *Brown* had to deal with an immense constitutional mess rooted in *Dred*-like judicial usurpation. It overturned the decision in *Plessy v. Ferguson*,[2] which held that states could require segregated train cars so long as their conditions were substantially equal. The *Plessy* court claimed that the equal protection of the laws guaranteed by the Fourteenth Amendment applied only to political rights (like voting) and not social rights like—well, there was the question. Court decisions maintaining this distinction in law entailed the kind of fact-finding and policy judgments the Constitution reserves for legislatures. What makes one train car (or public school) "equal" to another? How do we assure equality?

The *Brown* court could have recognized that such decisions aren't appropriate for a court and simply held that states can't enforce laws that categorize people according to race. After all, the Fourteenth Amendment was intended to end state actions denying African Americans' rights to due process and equal protection of the laws—that is, access to courts, fair trials, and equal treatment by state officials. Unfortunately, the court chose instead to keep making substantive decisions about what is equal or fair.

The *Brown* court struck down public school segregation as inherently unequal (because it involved stigmatizing African Americans). It didn't—couldn't—produce integrated public schools. Much as they have tried in recent decades, courts can't make people congregate and behave as we might want them to—at least not so long as ours remains a relatively free society. Decades of forced busing, court-ordered redrawing of district maps, control over intimate details of school policies, and even tax hikes to fund special programs empowered judges to act as legislators, administrators, and rulers; they also left public schools still separate and unequal. There was "massive resistance" to integration in many parts of the country; some based on racism, some based on parents' determination to keep their children in schools close to home, and some rooted in Americans' traditional refusal to simply bow to government dictates.

Civil rights actions outside the courts were more promising. Marches, rallies, and civil disobedience, along with brutal responses from local authorities, changed the conversation in America. The demand for opportunity and a new focus on character instead of skin color gained widespread support and, eventually, genuine civil rights reform. The Civil Rights Act of 1964 outlawed segregation in schools, employment, and public accommodations as well as biased enforcement of voter qualifications. It also went further, banning discrimination based on race, color, religion, sex, or national origin.

Conservatives by and large opposed the Civil Rights Act of 1964. Ever since, the claim has been that anyone who opposed any federal policy that claims to seek a more equal American people must be a racist. But conservatives didn't oppose the Civil Rights Act on account of racism. Barry Goldwater, Senator from Arizona, member of the NAACP and Urban League, conservative stalwart, and 1964 Republican presidential nominee, had supported previous civil rights legislation and fought for integration of the Phoenix public schools and the Arizona National Guard. Goldwater, and conservatives more generally, opposed any state action that discriminated on the basis of race. But they also opposed sections of the Civil Rights Act that empowered the federal government to determine who was and who was not discriminating in private and commercial relations. Americans, they thought, should be allowed to associate with whomever they choose without having to prove the virtue of their choices; they should not have to prove to the federal government that their businesses, their clubs, and their other associations were not discriminating on the basis of race. Or sex, for that matter. For sex, too, was now a category of federal concern.

Unfortunately, while the Civil Rights Act put an end to many morally corrupt practices, it included several provisions that helped establish increased federal control over Americans' private, commercial, and social lives. Over ensuing years, the federal government empowered its own agencies to police private associations and conduct. Federal agents would now decide what was fair and equal in American businesses, communities, voluntary associations, and, eventually, churches. They would put these associations on the defensive by presuming that any organization that failed to have the "right" number of members based in race or sex must be engaging in illegal discrimination. They would, in effect, reconfigure local associations to include "equal" representation by race and sex.

The demand for equality of conditions—of wealth and representation in schools, employment down to the level of specific jobs in specific companies, and various public and private arrangements—contradicts the traditional American commitment to opportunity. It's easy to muddy the waters, here, by referring to "equality of opportunity." But we can have fully equal opportunity only if we give government the power to reconfigure natural associations so that they will shape everyone "equally" into the kind of people whose opportunities will be equal. To do that we have to allow the government to ensure that everyone is given precisely the same upbringing, skills, and character. Historically, Americans have rejected such notions. They require a massive amount of intrusive government power. They also reject Americans' traditional understanding that equality is a presumption, and neither a goal nor a precondition. American equality has meant an absence of political and class distinctions. Historically, we've rejected any kind of aristocracy that gives separate rights and duties to people on account of their birth. That rejection makes for less inequality of condition because it undermines concentrations of power that can be used to help some and harm others as they pursue their own goals and interests. But it doesn't aim at equality of condition or even "opportunity." It aims at maintaining people's freedom to forge lives for themselves in their families and communities.

Martin Luther King's "I have a dream" speech was about judging people by character rather than skin color. If taken seriously, that vision means judging people by their course of action over time and how it reflects on whether they are good or bad husbands, wives, parents, children, employees, employers, and overall people. Judging institutions and associations to determine whether they are equal, on the other hand, is part of the judicial reconstruction of society. It sacrifices opportunity, and especially the opportunity of self-government, for equality as determined by experts. This is what the court demanded.

The court did much more to change American public life. The laissez-faire nineteenth-century court had taken to itself the power to redraft the constitution by finding in the Fourteenth Amendment an inalienable and all-but-unlimited right to freedom of contract. As it did in the *Dred Scott* case, the court spoke of rights the government could not violate under any conditions. FDR's New Deal had put this ideology to rest through threats of packing the Supreme Court and otherwise running over opposition to expanded federal power. Now, though, the court would renew its "substantive" campaign to control American politics under an even wider misinterpretation of the Fourteenth Amendment.

Using the doctrine of "substantive due process," Chief Justice Earl Warren and other members of the court declared that Americans enjoyed a vast number of "fundamental rights" the government could not violate unless the court found its reasons important enough to outweigh those rights. Where were these rights to be found? Some were in the constitution, some in the Bill of Rights, some in history; others, like privacy, resided in "emanations from penumbras" of rights found in these places.

One might expect all these new rights to make people freer, and especially less constrained by the power of the federal government. That's not what happened. Instead, courts pointed to these new rights as reasons why they could demand that the federal government "free" people from oppressions they suffered at the hands of their own states, townships, and associations. Society would have to be transformed so that people would be "free" from intrusions on their freedoms, their equality, their "rights" to everything from abortion (unfettered by, for example, parental consent), to taking their clothes off in bars for money (as a form of "expression"), to freedom from various forms of "discrimination" denying them equal possession of a variety of good things.

The Warren court handed down a host of decisions that decreed changes in the fundamental institutions of local life. Prayer was banished from public schools. Electoral maps were redrawn. And a new "right to privacy" was invoked to nullify laws regarding everything from abortion to same-sex marriage to the dissemination of pornography.

Progressivism was entering its next phase as legislatures increasingly were displaced by courts and executive agencies—the "experts" themselves—to reconstitute fundamental, natural associations. Equality had been a basic political presumption that was violated in order to leave out African

Americans. Now it would be the substantive goal of a veritable antidiscrimi-
nation state that would oversee all aspects of Americans' lives.

As to women, their employment opportunities had been limited, though
they had significantly widened over the course of the twentieth century. Now
federal law and policy not only further opened economic life to women, but
essentially forced millions of them into the workforce, whether they desired
paid employment or not. Before you scoff at that statement, consider this: In
2019, after decades of ideological and policy encouragement to work, Gallup
announced a "record high" 56 percent of women—only somewhat more than
half—preferred to work outside the home.[3] Even in recent years, then, almost
half of women refuse to "get with the program" of valuing career over family.
And they have valid reasons for their point of view.

For many decades, America's local associations, from church groups to
libraries, to charitable organizations, had benefited from women volunteers
who brought skills and passion to public service. Once employers learned
that any failure to have "enough" women on staff might bring discrimination
lawsuits, they moved to hire as many women as they could. The job market
was literally flooded during the 1960s and 1970s, lowering relative wages
for everyone, benefiting large businesses and undermining family culture
and economy.[4]

The positions women gained were, unfortunately, generally less than
rewarding. Often women had to apply for the very positions they once held as
volunteers. Only now these positions were low paying, dead-end jobs without
the honor and rewards of voluntary service. Many women had to take them
because their husbands could no longer make high enough wages to support
the family on their own. Many of these important local positions ceased to
exist altogether. Township life suffered, women were forced into an increasingly stifling, low-paid workforce, and children became more scarce and
more likely to be raised by government schools and daycare centers.

Change was in the offing. Change that would affect the very character of
Americans and their way of life. But the courts, whatever their claims and
desires, could only bring so much change. Resentment among those who
objected to court intrusions and those who thought change was coming too
slowly at times boiled over into violence. But the real change required something more than technocratic dictates from the courts. It would take cultural
movements. Such movements had secured one foundational change—the
Civil Rights Act of 1964. They would soon produce more. These movements
were more romantic than technocratic in their origins. To understand them we
first have to understand where they came from, namely, real flaws in our society that had much to do with the rise of a technocratic mindset that puts efficiency above decency. Unfortunately, when romance meets the facts of public
life, political power seems like the answer to make one's dream into reality.

NOTES

1. 347 U.S. 483 (1954).

2. 163 U.S. 537 (1896).

3. Megan Brenan, "Record-High 56% of U.S. Women Prefer Working to Home-making," Gallup, October 24, 2019, accessed June 9, 2022, https://news.gallup.com/poll/267737/record-high-women-prefer-working-homemaking.aspx.

4. John E. Schwartz, *America's Hidden Success: A Reassessment of Public Policy from Kennedy to Reagan* (New York: Norton, 1987).

Chapter 20

Radical Origins and Ideals

In 1962, Students for a Democratic Society (SDS) issued its Port Huron Statement. The Statement is a call to action filled with the trendy leftist jargon you would expect from undergraduates who've convinced themselves Mom and Dad learned nothing from surviving the Depression and winning a world war, and that only the wisdom gleaned from a coddled upbringing and a smattering of trendy leftist books can prepare you to transform the world. It contains few surprises, reading like a cross between a Socialist Party manifesto and a speech by Barack Obama. It's filled with platitudes about authenticity and community, mixed with plans to make everyone happy by having the federal government act as a massive community organizer, bringing people together to reconfigure economic and social life along collectivist lines—all somehow without the need for any police, regulation, or coercion of any kind.

But there is an element to the statement that might surprise you: it's filled with romantic longing. For example: "Loneliness, estrangement, isolation describe the vast distance between man and man today. These dominant tendencies cannot be overcome by better personnel management, nor by improved gadgets, but only when a love of man overcomes the idolotrous [sic] worship of things by man." And:

> We would replace power rooted in possession, privilege, or circumstance by power and uniqueness rooted in love, reflectiveness, reason, and creativity. As a social system we seek the establishment of a democracy of individual participation, governed by two central aims: that the individual share in those social decisions determining the quality and direction of his life; that society be organized to encourage independence in men and provide the media for their common participation.[1]

You can almost picture the statement's author (Tom Hayden, student radical leader and future husband to Jane Fonda), huddled over his typewriter in his mom's basement, looking longingly at a portrait of Lord Byron or a print from some Socialist Realist painting of heroic workers. But mockery is not the only appropriate reaction to these painfully earnest words. With all its pining for a sense of meaningful community the Statement tells us something about where the sixties came from. They came from the failures of the fifties.

The statement contains much criticism of the fifties that is, frankly, accurate. Universities had become faceless, soulless places for the mass production of graduates, the writing of profitable grants, and the smug declaration that "ideology is dead" such that all that is left is for progressive intellectuals to work out how to make democracy the best it can be. The statement of course puts a leftist spin on this reality. But the life of factory, corporation, and suburb had a definite downside to it, especially in its early years.

The real war in 1960s America was cultural. Prosperity, mass-produced consumer items, and vast increases in opportunities for travel and entertainment had spurred demand for ever-more stimulation at a time when these same forces had flattened out the culture, producing a sterility and sameness of architecture, town planning, and the design of public spaces. It's easy to dismiss these concerns as "merely aesthetic." But people require beauty, and they require opportunities to join with other people with whom they share common interests and characters if they are to form healthy associations and lead decent, relatively happy lives.

Betty Friedan's self-involved and overwrought talk of the suburbs as "comfortable concentration camps" had that small element of truth necessary to sell most falsehoods. The suburbs didn't have many real, large, and healthy trees yet. Suburban centers, where they existed, were still quite primitive and provided little of the social interaction a healthy domestic life in an advanced society requires. People who were happy to leave the dirt and crime of the city behind had forgotten to make sure their kids would have things to do once they were too old for playing house or building a makeshift dam on the local creek. As for wives and mothers, they had been disempowered by townships that engaged in relatively little self-government and were too divorced from urban problems to provide civic associations with enough meaningful work. Car culture was cool. But it wasn't enough for everyone. Sports were popular. Unfortunately, the warehouses that schools had become didn't have enough playing slots for most kids who wanted to participate. The Great Society programs that grew out of sixties critiques would make all this far worse, of course, but the critiques weren't baseless.

Boredom is no excuse for social destruction. But it's a partial explanation, especially when added to the self-reinforcing echo chamber of the Baby Boom, a vast cohort of well-off young people who literally created new markets for products, entertainment, and opinion. What's more, widespread coverage of civil rights abuses and a new emphasis on the problems of poverty now covered by the press had made America seem less beautiful and endearing, less capable of engaging the people's moral imagination.

Plenty of Americans remained or even became conservative. Two years before the Port Huron Statement, one hundred young conservatives met at the home of William F. Buckley to draft the Sharon Statement, which stands to this day as a seminal defense of ordered liberty, faith, and the traditional institutions of civic life. But a combination of press favoritism, world events like Vietnam, morally debilitating confusion over how best to address issues of civil rights, and elite pressure, especially from the Supreme Court, upended traditional American verities, creating a culture of self-doubt even as the counterculture challenged American society as a whole.

All this made young people especially susceptible to the calls of a simplistic form of progressivism. They rejected the talk of experts and managers, of course. But the call for "practical" change that would make the world more fair, safe, and conducive to individual choice all had power for young people who had been told from birth how great they were and how much they deserved a bright future at the same time that they found little interesting or engaging in their coddled lives. The Port Huron Statement, and the movement that owed so much to the ideology it proclaimed, tried hard to ground its cultural angst in concrete complaints and proposals. In true progressive fashion, the statement rejects history and tradition in favor of a plan of action rooted in two motivating "facts": "the permeating and victimizing fact of human degradation, symbolized by the Southern struggle against racial bigotry" and "the enclosing fact of the Cold War, symbolized by the presence of the Bomb," which "brought awareness that we ourselves, and our friends, and millions of abstract 'others' we knew more directly because of our common peril, might die at any time."

In other words, concrete facts like Jim Crow were just "symbols" of abstractions like "degradation" that could be applied whenever and however Students for a Democratic Society chose—as it turned out against all forms of inequality. Normal Americans were blamed for "otherizing" strangers by not pretending we know enough to take responsibility for their well-being. SDS repackaged one of progressivism's abiding themes: the moral enormity of inequality, here "symbolized" by the concrete reality of racism, and the need for political actors to channel the people's will into a powerful state that would tend to their needs. They then emphasized the fear of annihilation that would gain them converts, media coverage, and a decades-long reputation for both idealism and common sense that were as destructive as they were undeserved. They would harness the power of fear (even auguring today's climate hysteria) to drive Americans toward a more centralized, state-driven way of life.

Fear of apocalypse was very real during the Cold War. "Duck and cover" drills were omnipresent, as were books, movies, and newspaper columns predicting the end of the world in a nuclear holocaust. The World War II generation had experience dealing stoically with the possibility of death. Stoicism was in short supply among their children. Then America entered the Vietnam War and young people had a more immediate threat to life and limb to contend with. And some of the critiques had a point. Wonder Boy Hoover had been replaced by "the best and the brightest"—whiz kids from Harvard who thought they could run the war in Vietnam from their offices in Washington. And, after years of sending young men to meaningless deaths in foreign jungles, these elitists still couldn't admit that perhaps their business school charts and calculations hadn't made for a winning strategy. The draft and especially the eventual trimming of student deferments created a harmonic convergence of idealism and self-preservation praised in the media and resented by the mostly working-class Americans who did their duty as they saw it. Calls to "ban the bomb" and accept that we were "Better Red than Dead" echoed throughout the student movement.

Marches, riots, and general chaos followed. But the problem was not that America was divided during the 1960s and 1970s. Americans have always been divided. The problem was that the 1960s generation would achieve enough power to undermine the common assumptions and associations on which our common culture and character were based.

For good or ill, the violence and disruptions of the 60s were its least remarkable element. We Americans have always been divided. We were made from and for conflict. Immigrants from a variety of often-hostile home countries, our forebears conquered a continent (sparsely) occupied by often warring tribes. They settled in isolated communities within what became semi-sovereign states under the loose umbrella of a distinctly limited federal government.

We've always joined with our neighbors for the common good. As a nation? Not so much. We haven't even been all that united in our wars. Some of our forebears were revolutionary loyalists, some were near-secessionist New Englanders opposing the War of 1812, some were followers of future President Lincoln opposing the War with Mexico, some were combatants on either (or both) sides of a Civil War, and some were even "suspect" Americans whose foreign-language newspapers and associations Woodrow Wilson felt justified suppressing on account of World War I. In peacetime, too, our conflicts kept us divided, as well as free and self-governing.

Once the Japanese attacked Pearl Harbor, World War II was different. And after America won this truly global war against obvious aggressors, we soon faced a new threat: expansive, belligerent Soviet Communism. The enemy was godless at a time when most Americans remained deeply committed to their faith and to a Christian form of life, collectivist at a time when Americans were finally enjoying prosperity and mobility again, and massively militarist at a time when Americans yearned for a return to sweet isolation without the burden of a standing army.

The Cold War was more contested than many people today believe. But few openly sided with the Soviets. The spies who gave the atom bomb to Stalin acted in secret. The progressive left focused on criticizing anti-communists, rather than defending communism itself. Thanks to old Soviet records, we now know that there were, in fact, hundreds of Soviet spies in the federal government, with many more in important positions within unions and the media.[2] But the total number was small and Senator Joseph McCarthy's clumsy, bullying tactics in public hearings backfired, helping establish the story that American freedoms were under assault less from Soviet Communism than from superpatriot Americans and anyone else in a position of authority.

Sixties protests, drug-addled orgies, and appalling fashion sense all added to a general atmosphere of rebellion against authority, as did the emphasis on subjecting every aspect of life to the democratic process. Moreover, the radicals seemed to demand an end to "the system" run by experts left over from the New Deal. But the radicals really were demanding a further extension of that New Deal—it would become a "New Frontier" under John F. Kennedy and, far more destructively, a Great Society under Lyndon Johnson. As ever, the "nonconformist" left was all about tearing down existing institutions to make room for themselves to take positions of power and authority.

NOTES

1. *The Port Huron Statement,* Students for a Democratic Society, accessed June 9, 2022, http://www.progressivefox.com/misc_documents/PortHuronStatement.pdf.

2. Herbert Romerstein, *The Venona Secrets: Exposing Soviet Espionage and America's Traitors* (Washington, DC: Regnery, 2014).

Chapter 21

Conflicting Visions

The 1960s served as a watershed for American politics and character. That destructive time (actually from about 1962 until the mid-1970s) separated Americans in deep and entirely new ways. The "counterculture" was, indeed, a culture that ran counter to the mainstream of American mores. Because of it, Americans' political differences have gone beyond disagreements over what policies would best serve our people in their communities to whether and how "we"—meaning powerful political actors—can use government and law to fundamentally change politics, society, and our character itself.

These changes didn't come from nowhere. And they weren't produced by some cabal of foreign intellectuals who seduced young Americans with neo-Marxist social criticism. Like the plants so many youth leaders smoked, the 1960s were largely homegrown. Part narcissistic youth culture, part nouveau-riche idealism, and part fear of boredom and destruction, the 1960s were, more than anything else, a triumph of progressivism. They didn't produce their promised utopia but did establish a vast "social justice" bureaucracy that undermined local associations (especially the family) and subjected Americans to unprecedented federal regulation. The rebels who claimed to fight "the system" soon burrowed their way into its universities, media empires, and administrative state. From these positions, they and their progeny have worked ever since to substitute bureaucratic structures (run by "enlightened" administrators) for natural associations, tradition, religion, and stoic virtues and to teach Americans to despise their traditional character and way of life.

The real target was Main Street. Mocked for generations by progressives for its provincial boosterism, the local public square always had been crucial to American life. In it people would meet one another at their self-conscious best. They would dress, speak, and behave in a manner suitable for public consumption. Here they would conduct business, worship, and gather in patriotic, civic, and religious celebrations throughout the year. Here they would set and strive to live up to public standards of virtue.

161

The American town made no pretensions to moral perfection. Vice and sin could be found, and sometimes would find you. But most folk sought to live up to standards rooted in common religious beliefs, and to be respectable. That meant behaving well, especially on the public streets. In new settlements these standards were hard to maintain. The church and the schoolhouse had to contend with the saloon. But local boosters and civic and religious leaders worked hard to limit the saloon's influence and eventually to banish it to the back streets, handing over its prime spot to a fine hotel where more elevated standards could rule.

If this all sounds stuffy, boring, and unrealistic, keep in mind that our towns and cities were constantly working to keep order among a habitually unruly people. Public standards didn't rule everywhere. But they could be upheld reasonably well on Main Street so that public unity could be supported and, in its turn, support a public spirit conducive to a flourishing community life. Progressive reformers had attacked the mix of activities on Main Street before, seeking to get rid of the saloon altogether, for example. At the same time, of course, newer immigrants worked to keep the neighborhood bar close to, if not on, Main Street. Then again, their neighborhood bars rarely included a brothel upstairs. The balance of forces essential for ordered liberty survived well into the 1960s and abides even today in many small towns and maintained a sense of self-respect among and for the community—that boosterism so maligned today was born of a sense of both self and common ownership of the streets, shops, and associations, encouraging everyone to support, clean, and participate in what was deeply their own.

1960s radicals rejected an ordered public square in favor of an arena of personal expression and conflict. Occasional riots we had had from the beginning. The radicals wanted to normalize unrest. Rejecting decency as a form of oppression, they championed individual expression and authenticity. They brought a good deal of disorder and violence. But what made them largely successful was an elite campaign, carried out mostly by the courts, to create a new value utterly foreign to American history and character: privacy.

You probably find that last statement bizarre. Privacy is un-American? We're overstating matters a bit for effect but, yes, Americans before the 1960s most decidedly did not think in terms of protecting their privacy. This is not to say that no Americans wanted to be free from public examination. But if they did, they had one (and only one) essential means of achieving that goal: land. A fair number of Americans had literally gone insane from the "privacy" they got by being planted on isolated plots of land during the heyday of homesteading. But land certainly provided the independence Americans valued so highly. This had never meant pure privacy because the American household often included both an extended family and dependent laborers. And it generally did not include much in the way of household privacy, what with the lack of bathrooms (an overused outhouse is not a place to enjoy a bit of private reading) or private bedrooms. In town, remember, most people didn't even have curtains on their front parlor windows. One wouldn't want the neighbors to think you were hiding something.

The fact that so many of us cringe at the thought of such public display shows how far we've come over the last several decades toward a different kind of culture. But is this progress? Or a loss of confidence in the decency and respect of ourselves and our neighbors? Now that most of us don't have (or certainly use) a front porch, do we enjoy life more? Or do we simply fear neighbors who have become strangers?

What we now term privacy began as a set of protections against government coercion that were ensconced in the Bill of Rights. The Constitution forbade the federal government, as the common law forbade state and local governments, from beating down doors (or beating citizens) to find or manufacture evidence against them. The government couldn't dig through Americans' papers and records or throw us in jail until they could figure out some crime to charge us with. Our neighbors? They couldn't trespass on our property. These rights protected our independence.

Over time, though, the courts created a new set of rights intended to protect rich and important people from the prying eyes of the public and especially the press. This "right to privacy" was created by and for elites. Later courts would claim it was an emanation from penumbras in the Constitution, whatever that means. But its real source was an 1890 *Harvard Law Review* article, cowritten by future Supreme Court justice Louis Brandeis, arguing that America should change its laws to create a "right to be let alone."[1] This "right," which originated with rich people's umbrage at newspaper gossip columns discussing their doings, was harnessed by social activists to undermine laws aimed at maintaining public decorum and to support the natural family. Public fornication, abortion, and marriage itself were turned into "private" choices neither government nor public could oversee.

Before you cringe too much, we should remind you that very few people thought laws in these "private" realms were preventing all forms of vice— even the ones most Americans take for granted today. Couples still found places to have pre- or extramarital sex, for example. They just couldn't openly register together at a hotel to do it. In a lot of cities prostitution itself was legal. But civic leaders and normal folk were determined to limit it and, especially, keep it off the streets. And at the time the law was on their side. Now of course our "free" society forbids us to bat an eye at public cohabitation and Home and Garden Television runs episodes of *House Hunters* featuring a "throuple" (a man and two girlfriends, with children). Progress is defined as open disdain for traditional morality, natural associations, and protecting children from being sexualized.

The Supreme Court began declaring major changes in laws dealing with morals, declaring "private" and so matters of mere personal choice the kinds of conduct that make or break families and other fundamental relationships. The real effect was less to leave individuals alone than to force communities to let individuals parade their choices in public. The hippies certainly weren't about privacy; they wanted to let it all hang out. Sixties radicals valued their self-expression, particularly as a way to thumb their noses at the normals. More generally, sixties activists insisted that the right to offend was somehow essential to American liberty. It wasn't. Free speech always had been understood as aimed primarily at fostering public debate. Intentionally offending people by calling the Mother of their Lord a prostitute was considered illegal (a breach of the peace)[2] as well as unwise, and pornography, while available to those who sought it out, was generally kept off Main Street, and certainly would not have been beamed into children's smartphones.

But, ever since the Supreme Court declared that only speech presenting a "clear and present danger" could be banned, a more individualistic ethic had grown. By the 1960s it became common for activists to burn flags, draft cards, and the like, to wear T-shirts emblazoned with vulgar words and sayings, and to expose themselves in various ways in public. They intended to offend but somehow this was taken as largely protected self-expression. In a nation known for vigorous debate over public issues, it became acceptable to short-circuit reasoned discussion by insulting and even assaulting people with whom you disagreed. We've been paying an increasing price for this corruption of free speech ever since.

A host of Supreme Court decisions "freed" individuals from community standards. Thousands of people with mental problems were freed from deeply troubled and even cruel mental institutions, for example. But they weren't put into decent, humane institutions. Instead, they were dumped on the streets to join addicts and vagrants flooding the public square with aggressive panhandling, erratic, often frightening and even violent behavior. The most extreme of these actions weren't, and aren't, protected even by current Supreme Court doctrine but they are protected by various local governments trapped by the ideology of individual expression. The rest of us must simply put up with everything from public drug use to public defecation and squalor, forbidden to join together to provide real help because our public authorities, such as they are, have come to see the autonomy of self-destructive people as more important than our pursuit of a decent community. Riots, spiking murder rates, and massive "smash and grab" robberies naturally followed.

A key element preventing communities from helping the troubled on their streets is a concept central to the 1960s, namely, authenticity. Sixties radicals valued self-expression above all else. But the self that was expressed had to be authentic. No outside pressures, no coercion, no influence from the dead hand of the past or the establishment could be allowed. This was what the attack on authority was all about—undermining old, traditional standards in favor of 60s radicals' standards of individual autonomy and authenticity. Nowhere was this rather odd belief in self-creation and narcissistic insistence on sincerity as somehow the be-all and end-all virtue more damaging than on Main Street. It delegitimized all the ceremonies that bound communities together and changed local self-rule to rule by hecklers and mobs.

But no society can be truly neutral. Some general ethic, be it civilized or barbaric, self-governing or imposed, will prevail. And so, over time, new arbiters of public morals coalesced around the "virtue" of perpetually taking offense. And so today we see claims of "hate speech" and "disinformation" used to stifle traditional values and dissent from current orthodoxies.

Building this new orthodoxy began with an assault aimed principally at religion. Prayer in schools, local nativity pageants, and other community expressions of religious faith were attacked as somehow oppressive because nonbelievers and dissidents were "forced" to endure the spectacle. Justice Antonin Scalia made this point in dissenting from a later opinion branding "unconstitutional" a nondenominational prayer delivered by a rabbi at a middle school graduation ceremony: "the Court—with nary a mention that it is doing so—lays waste a tradition that is as old as public school graduation ceremonies themselves, and that is a component of an even more longstanding American tradition of nonsectarian prayer to God at public celebrations generally. As its instrument of destruction, the bulldozer of its social engineering, the Court invents a boundless, and boundlessly manipulable, test of psychological coercion."[3]

As Scalia was no doubt aware, the issue was less one of coercion for the court than of intentionally destroying local communities' ability to express religious opinions nonbelievers might find offensive. The 1960s set in motion a cultural revolution rooted in disgust with traditional America and devoted to tearing down its pillars of authority: Christianity, the natural family, and local authority—faith, family, and local self-government. But the revolution could not be accomplished without massive governmental support. The results have been cataclysmic for our national character.

NOTES

1. Samuel Warren and Louis Brandeis, "The Right to Privacy," 4 *Harvard Law Review* 193 (1890).
2. See for example *People v. Ruggles*, 8 Johns. 290 (1811).
3. *Lee v. Weisman*, 505 U.S. 577 (1992).

Chapter 22

Administrative Centralization
and Its Effects

It's fair to say 1960s radicalism brought political change. Most dramatically, riots and demonstrations literally burned down and emptied cities like Detroit, chased Lyndon Johnson from power, and made continuation of the (misbegotten) war in Vietnam untenable. But "street action" can only tear down. On its own it can't build or transform institutions. For that the radicals of the sixties relied on the same federal government they'd condemned. In fact, many of them joined that government, at one level or another, to impose the kinds of change they sought.

Those changes were aimed at "freeing" Americans from traditional families, churches, and local associations. These fundamental institutions might survive, but they would no longer dominate the public square; they would no longer be able to shape many Americans' characters. Now various government agencies and administrators would exercise control over each of them, reducing their power and reconfiguring them to serve their own ends. The result would be an increasing number of Americans who have never known a full, intact family, who are unchurched, and whose experience of local association is minimal and has less to do with self-government than with demanding that someone else—generally the federal government—govern with greater vigor. The mechanism of this change was the combination of federal programs and initiatives called the Great Society.

We all live in the Great Society, or at least the Great Society world that LBJ built. We do not live here because the administrative state defines all of America, let alone all of the American character. We live here because the Great Society, and the myth that sustains it, draw the battle lines of a culture war that has shaped American public life for at least two generations.

LBJ ended his career and life in disgrace. Over the decades his lies, corruption, hypocrisy, and simple brutishness became clear to all but the most biased observers. Not so his bureaucratic legacy. Even as the horrendous impact of the welfare, administrative, and anti-discrimination monoliths have emerged, questioning the grand structures of the Great Society has become tantamount to political, professional, and social suicide. You say our welfare state fosters dependency? You want poor people to starve. You say our administrative state stifles freedom and innovation? You want faceless corporations to poison our children. You think government and government-backed lawsuits forcing American employers and folks renting out rooms to "prove" they aren't bigots have undermined social relations, impeded African American advancement, and worsened the racial tensions their promoters claimed they would improve? You are a straight-up racist.

These are the articles of faith, enforced by government, elite opinion, and social media, that insulate the managerial class that runs our centralized administrative institutions from effective criticism. Thus, for decades, the structures set up by LBJ have been extended and consolidated with little effective resistance. And so the Great Society grew to the point of changing our constitutional order and even the character of a substantial portion of the American people.

The political and administrative history from this point is a predictable playing out of the Great Society. From Nixon's "Great Society Lite" of big government agencies and programs to the Carter Administration's Great Malaise of hyperregulation at home and humiliation on the world stage, the 1970s saw the entrenchment of the feckless but insistent bureaucratic mindset. It also saw the spread of this mindset and its structures into an increasing number of American lives as it fed on its own failures. Spiking crime, disintegrating families, multigenerational welfare dependency, and rampant drug abuse were only the most obvious products of an expanding centralized state. But even as it caused these problems, the federal government fostered calls for greater centralization by teaching Americans to trust "experts," fear one another, and reject their traditions.

Customary relations and traditional social trust were openly attacked. Local associations were deemed discriminatory for favoring preexisting ties of friendship. Lawsuits became the favored means of settling disputes from arguments over damaged goods to debates over public policies. It was as if the Old West duel was now to be fought with checkbooks and lawyers, as the law's "adversarial system" turned disputants into ciphers who hired others to game the system instead of fighting their own battles. The cult status of "rebel" meant that reputation for honesty and fair dealing came to seem the realm of suckers and hucksters. And increasing numbers of Americans became enamored of the notion that any instance of unfairness or even misfortune is unjust and must be corrected through federal action.

Not everyone followed this trajectory, of course. Traditional American character and institutions still held sway among most Americans. After opting out of politics in favor of home and religious life for decades, evangelical Christians reentered politics especially on account of court assaults on public displays of religion and on private morality in the family. They scored electoral successes that promised change, culminating in the election of Ronald Reagan. But the Reagan years, while they produced victory in the Cold War (no small achievement) barely slowed the spread of the administrative state. Worse, in the 1980s administrators in government, on campus, and in corporate human resource departments launched the next phase of progressive revolution: diversity politics. Former 1960s radicals within various bureaucracies worked to manipulate civil rights rules to require "representation" of minority groups over merit and social cohesion. At the same time, members of these very minority groups, increasingly bereft of strong, intact families and flourishing natural associations, suffered increasing violence, crime, and hopelessness.

Reagan's optimism and faith in American individualism presented a breath of fresh air to millions of traditional Americans. But it was only a breath, not a return to the free and decentralized atmosphere from before the Great Society. Instead, the Reagan years began a massive shift toward corporate globalization. Government agents and corporate cronies replaced "trade agreements" with trade managed by and for themselves, sacrificing workers to lower prices and higher profits and barriers to entry by small, innovative businesses. To this was added an astonishing series of foreign adventures conducted under both parties in the name of a kind of "creative destruction" at home and abroad that aimed to turn every nation into a cheap copy of the United States.

Managers in government and large corporations outsourced formerly high-paying working-class jobs. This, of course, brought greater dependence on government handouts, demoralizing citizens who were once central to American economic and social life. The same managers continually expanded and reoriented immigration. From a program aimed at bringing in people who could make a contribution to American economic life immigration was turned into another program aimed at "diversifying" America while aiding the corporate bottom line. Immigrants, instead of being encouraged to settle in America as Americans, were offered increasing federal assistance, educated away from assimilation, and, in many cases, kept in segregated, disadvantaged work situations that kept them under the thumb of employers. We are thinking especially of migrant and tech workers brought in under special visas or allowed to remain more-or-less illegally so that they were not in a position to give their employers trouble, though they might be eligible for certain government benefits. The result has been a degradation of the very Americans on whom our character depended: people of modest means but pride and self-government in their local associations.

As the people were being demoralized and replaced, the constitutional order was being deconstructed along with our understanding of the Constitution and even of what it means to be ruled by law. Increasingly, Americans had to look out for and obey regulations coming from a variety of agencies, court orders with no clear basis in anything other than the will of some judge, and the mere declarations of presidents (and governors) for the rules by which we must live. Congress now merely passed vague directives to administrators to "make the air clean" or "eliminate discrimination." The real work of making people change their behavior was delegated to administrators who could change their definitions of good and bad conduct at any time and who, effectively, could not be challenged.[1]

This is not the constitutional order of a self-governing people. What's more, it allowed the growth of institutions and policies that undermined the natural, fundamental associations in which Americans learned *how* to be a self-governing people. We often are told that the breakdown of the family, the decreasing practice of religion, and the dwindling interest in local associations are the natural results of modernization. These claims aren't credible, especially when they come from people who have spent their careers intentionally undermining them. If we look even briefly at federal policies on families (including welfare policies as well as marriage rules), at the treatment of religion in recent decades, and at the overall centralization of government power, it is obvious that changes in American institutions and the growth of a separate, nontraditional American character are the intentional results of federal policy. Progressive ideology sought to separate people from local associations in the name of national ideological goals—"social justice"—and they at least partially succeeded.

Charles Murray, among others, has shown the utter failure of welfare policy to bring Americans out of poverty.[2] At least as important, however, has been the impact of these programs on the institutions that once helped people who are poor in terms of their income to live decently and raise their children with the hope of better lives. Our settler forebears were extremely poor in material terms. But they had reasonable hope that they could earn themselves a better and even a very good life through hard work within their families and townships. Welfare policies that subsidize out-of-wedlock births and no-fault divorce, along with education policies that stigmatize traditional families have, not unexpectedly, sapped the family's strength.

Families were the places where Americans formed good character in their children and maintained it among adults. Today, those families break down or fail to form at an astounding rate. For example, in 1960 3.8 percent of American babies were born to unmarried mothers. In 2010 that number was almost 41 percent, so that "Approximately 36 percent of the American generation born from 1993 through 2012 . . . were born to unmarried mothers."[3]

Clearly the moral stigma of illegitimacy has been reduced. At the same time, however, no one any longer disputes the connection between illegitimacy and various forms of dependency on government agencies. Children without intact families are denied important, formative resources for their development and so must fight harder if they are to become self-governing adults.

Religion also once helped people deal with and work themselves out of material poverty. Not merely "spirituality" in some abstract sense, but religion, whose root meaning is "to bind," provided in-person charity and encouragement to help poor people—and others—improve their lives. They also helped teach the virtues necessary for happy, meaningful, and successful lives. Their rituals and community activities gave a pattern to local life that reinforced democratic as well as family and Christian values and bound people to one another in community. For decades now, religion has been officially banned in large swaths of our society and mocked or ignored in others; the public square has been made naked of religion. Again, not surprisingly, the campaign has had its effects. Church membership among Americans has dropped from over 70 percent as recently as 1983 to only 50 percent today. This means that only half of Americans are "churched" in the sense that their lives are structured in significant measure by common religious practices, customs, and relationships.[4] The rest glean their values and moral habits from secular institutions like public schools, the media, or peers—themselves often also unchurched and from broken families.

More generally, local associations in America are a shadow of their former selves. Perhaps the most famous work on this subject is Robert Putnam's *Bowling Alone*,[5] which quantifies the steep decline in Americans' membership in local associations from self-governing townships to bowling leagues. But Robert Nisbet more than seventy years ago pointed out the central reason local associations are dying: their role in people's daily lives has been taken over by centralized bureaucratic organizations. Without these associations, individual liberty will die along with social life. But they can flourish only if they have something to do; something beyond bowling—namely, self-government.[6]

The increasing dominance of a managerial elite in American politics has encouraged as it has been encouraged by a technocratic politics hostile to American self-government. Again, often confused with an inevitable process of modernization, the demand that politics be "efficient" in producing more "fair" results increasingly has been put forward as the perpetual, inevitable goal of all democratic people. This hasn't been the case among Americans. But it has among our managers within both political parties. Thus, the fight over centralization hasn't fallen out neatly along partisan lines.

Both political parties have eagerly pursued progressive governance. We could write a book (in fact, we did[7]) on the failure of the American conservative movement to address our people's loss of self-government since the Great Society. And people from many walks of life have found themselves increasingly dependent on the centralized administration that undermines their communities' very reason to exist: from farmers demanding both free-dom and crop subsidies to inner city churches fighting for faith and family while they and their congregations depend on a host of bureaucratic structures for jobs, financial assistance, and the illusion of political power. The promise of progressivism—freedom from insecurity and the feeling that one has been treated unfairly—comes at the cost of destroying the intermediary associa-tions that are the heart and shape the soul of a self-governing people.

NOTES

1. Bruce P. Frohnen and George W. Carey, *Constitutional Morality and the Rise of Quasi-Law* (Cambridge: Harvard University Press, 2016), ch. 6.

2. See especially his *Losing Ground: American Social Policy 1950–1980* (New York: Basic Books, 2015).

3. Terence Jeffrey, "Surge in welfare stems from rise in out-of-wedlock births," *Washington Examiner*, September 3, 2014, accessed June 9, 2022, https://www .washingtonexaminer.com/surge-in-welfare-stems-from-rise-in-out-of-wedlock -births.

4. Jeffrey M. Jones, "U.S. Church Membership Down Sharply in Past Two Decades," Gallup, April 18, 2019, accessed June 9, 2022, https://news.gallup.com/ poll/248837/church-membership-down-sharply-past-two-decades.aspx.

5. Robert A. Putnam, *Bowling Alone: The Collapse and Revival of American Com-munity* (New York: Simon & Schuster, 2000).

6. Robert A. Nisbet, *The Quest for Community: A Study in the Ethics of Order and Freedom* (Wilmington: ISI, 2010).

7. Ted V. McAllister and Bruce P. Frohnen, *Coming Home: Reclaiming America's Conservative Soul* (New York: Encounter, 2019).

Chapter 23

Two Peoples, Two Americas?

Decades of deepening progressivism made possible the election of a political neophyte, a former "community organizer" and acolyte of revolutionary agitators like Saul Alinsky, as president. But it would be wrong to see in Barack Obama any radical break with the past. Just as Obama himself was no foreign agent as some on the alt-right still claim, so his ideology was no foreign, Marxist import from abroad. The "fundamental transformation" Obama promised to his followers was rooted in the progressivism growing in our midst for over a century.

Obama worked around and undermined our constitutional system as best he could to finish the structures of a social democratic state. The transformation he sought in government- run healthcare didn't fully materialize because Americans remained allergic to overt forms of socialism. But Obamacare has managed to expand our slide toward a corrupt system in which huge corporations (in this instance insurance companies and mega-hospitals) join with bureaucrats to micromanage both consumers (patients) and providers (doctors), bringing exploding costs and collapsing services. All in the name of fairness, as judged by our elites.

Obama, elected in the hope of racial reconciliation, produced yet more conflict through his commitment to a world in which the United States would side with "liberation movements" at home and abroad. All this while further empowering community organizers to reeducate children and adults into an ideology hostile to family, faith, and tradition. Obama's policies were a natural progression of those instituted by presidents from Wilson to LBJ. Even the New Left ideas Obama sometimes promoted owed more to the American leftism of experts "managing" democracy than to the Marxist screeds emanating from many of the foreign movements he championed.

The result was not a harsh totalitarian regime. It was a softer, more "inclusive" movement toward mob rule centered in social media and university life, along with a hectoring rule by elites committed to "nudging" people into the "right" behavior. Intricate public policies tied to ever-expanding entitlement payments were designed to reconfigure our decision making to make it more politically correct and, in contemporary terms wiser, because far more risk averse and pliant. All would be based in a doctrine of material equality for all those who would be governed by the managerial elite who keep a watchful eye over them through CCTV cameras and various oversight boards with the right to rifle through their public and formerly private papers and electronic messages.

Progressive government didn't produce the abundance, efficiency, and loyalty to the people's will it promised. It did, however, make America's into a different kind of government and making many Americans a different kind of people. Decades of working for "social justice" have solidified a managerial class and a growing class of people dependent on it and its programs. It is tempting to talk of this new arrangement as the birth of a European-style society. Much wished for among Progressives for many years, this society is one of classes and orders far more stringent and guarded than traditional America.[1] It is populated by people who define themselves by their status within a hierarchy of power and prestige as ruler or ruled. The nature of this duality is somewhat blurred by the demands of the ruled for material goods and signs of recognition from their rulers. Still, those goods are delivered, not through self-governing associations, but through management of the administrative machinery that orders taxpayers, employers, churches, clubs, and others to provide them as dictated by administrators.

The character of these Americans is different from that of their forebears. It values "inclusion," not independence, "self-expression" not honor, gratification not discipline, end results not the unending process of self-government and community flourishing. Among these Americans, rulers and ruled are bound together, not by any deal among equals who share power, but through a transaction whereby the rulers provide the goods for the ruled in exchange for quiet acceptance of their dictates. The people, now, may be unruly through crime, riots, and the occasional demonstration but are, in fact, no longer their own masters in their daily lives.

The new Americans are not the only Americans. The 2016 and 2020 presidential elections showed that our country is roughly evenly divided along cultural lines. Donald Trump, pugnacious and determined to Make America Great Again in terms of international respect, domestic prosperity, and subjugation of elites and the administrative state to a lost constitutional consensus, was painted as a throwback to an oppressive era in which white males ruled America with iron fists. In reality, Trump was propelled into the White House by many of the same people who had supported Ronald Reagan, fought for tax cuts over decades, and Marched for Life. Trump added to this coalition an increasing number of Americans of all faiths and races—many former Obama voters—who had been victimized by globalization and who increasingly recognized that they had been cast adrift from the normal human relationships that make life worth living in an advanced technological society. The question was whether that coalition could stand, work together, and support a national program that aimed, not merely to make the nation itself great, but to tame the nation-state and return it to its proper role of guarding rather than running the communities in which Americans actually lived.

Elites in both parties and, most importantly, throughout the managerial classes in government, media, and corporate America declared all-out war on Trump even before he came to office. Four years of conspiracy theories about Russian interference, promoted as news by both the press and many within the administrative state, led to impeachment and empowered administrators to challenge Trump at every turn. Vicious "public health" lockdowns and massive voter fraud, abetted by courts that refused to hear evidence (and by the president's failure to move against deep state opponents in his own administration), brought Trump's presidency to an end, at least for now, and with it any effective resistance to the next phase of administrative centralization—a phase not even Obama dared hope to make real.

That phase would build on the worst of progressivism, within a system ruled by brahmin bureaucrats, unchecked by a figurehead president, who seek to follow the lead of a tiny number of radical activists who reject any connection with our traditions in favor of an ideology rooted superficially in trendy postmodern academic jargon but mostly in the will to power. The demand that statues be torn down, whether they represent Confederate generals, early American statesmen, or Abraham Lincoln, are more than merely reminiscent of the French Revolutionary mobs that sacked churches and murdered priests, nuns, and anyone else who attempted to stand in their way. Armed bands of "anti-fascists" have beaten demonstrators and worked to burn down police stations and courthouses. "Black Lives Matter" activists have encouraged violence and called for race-based boycotts. Asians especially have been targeted for beatings and even murder. Government figures from Congress to the local prosecutors' offices have praised the mobs and empowered through inaction and policies "defunding the police." Refusing to protect "deplorable" adversaries from violence, our managerial elites and their enablers among the faculties, human resource departments, and Twitter mobs seek to discipline those who until recently were recognized as normal, hardworking, decent Americans. Not even the courts are now immune from mob intimidation as the recent "doxing" of Supreme Court justices voting "wrong" on the issue of abortion have been surrounded by crowds with the blessing of the current administration. Having taken the commanding heights of our culture, this new class, sharing little with the rest of us, already has fundamentally transformed many Americans' character and now seeks to transform the rest of us, if not into "woke" partisans, then at least into weak peasants.

Within American culture the story has been constant, increasingly hate-filled conflict, a divide having been drawn between those who are attached to American traditions and those who attack our traditional way of life as a racist, sexist, homophobic tool of "big money interests." Often painted in ugly, racial terms, the conflict actually has spanned racial divides, pitting people committed to the decentralized, locality-based culture that once dominated in the United States against those committed to a globalist, social democratic culture of centralized administration and individual dependence on the state.

In this book we have tried to spell out some of the reasons why this happened—from the dislocations of industrialization to the rigors of war, to the resentments of genuine wrongs and the illusions of ideology. A combination of technocrats in government, media, and business seek to finalize a new society. In this society the people are wards of managers and administrators. The Biden presidency does not bode well for the competency of the resulting regime. Indeed, the kind of managerial state they are seeking to finish and entrench is producing the same results in the United States as in every other country, from the former Soviet Union to the current Venezuela, that has tried it. Stagflation, dislocation, and violence at home, humiliation abroad, and a general malaise take root and progress to the point where the choices come down to tyranny or an end to the new regime.

The humiliating, cowardly fiasco of the great lockdowns and mask mandates of 2020–2021 is the reductio ad absurdum of the new, "expert" mindset. On the basis of "science" born of guesswork plugged into computer models and aided by postapocalyptic literature and movies, supposedly free people abandoned their elders to deadly, genuinely virus-infected nursing homes while cowering in their basements, waiting for contactless deliveries and direct deposits of their government checks. They (and their religious leaders) even submitted as they were ordered to forgo church services while rioters roamed the streets of their major cities.

Americans had been working up to this failure of nerve for decades. Millions of them already had abandoned community self-government for federal action and hecklers' vetoes in many aspects of their common lives. Millions of Americans bowed before the power of the state and its public health "experts," at first out of fear of an unknown virus, then out of fear for of being "canceled" and stripped of their jobs and social standing. Worst of all, no public debate was allowed. Government and social media simply deplatformed dissenters—something rare in American history and deadly to a free people. And millions more Americans took to the new, masked reality almost with relief, finding comfort in their isolation and reliance on others to keep them safe.

These new Americans coexist uncomfortably and at times unpeacefully with a large swath of traditional Americans, mostly in the less-urban areas, who remain committed to a life of local self-government. Rather than repeat what we've already said of this character or expand on the new one we merely point out, here, that these two characters are, in the long run, incompatible. Especially given the breakdown of our constitutional structure, it is highly unlikely that any nation can survive long term so divided in its characters and fundamental assumptions regarding what makes for a good society and a good life.

Democracy means literally rule by the many. Historically it has meant unstable, selfish, and unthinking rule by a mob. In the United States it meant something quite different. Early observers of our country marveled that it could survive as a free republic without an aristocracy. "Wiser heads must rule" has been the slogan of elites from the ancient Greeks to modern progressives. The only difference concerned who was "wise"—the well-born or the well-credentialed. For more than two hundred years, as colonists and citizens, Americans ruled themselves without an aristocracy because they were not that other class so often associated with aristocratic regimes: peasants. American farmers belonged to no master and, while indentured servants and slaves lived among them (or in other states) the model of citizenship was fixed early and firmly: the settler, head of household, yeoman, independent man of business who took responsibility to educate himself about the public good and its requirements.

Democratic—that is, free from hard class lines—in their culture, Americans have been republican or self-governing in their political and social lives. But only a people with the character of a free people—the habits and the determination to be free—can in fact be self-governing. What is needed is a specific kind of self-governing, republican virtue. Republican virtue in America was common virtue. Only when the associations of republican life—the township and its fundamental elements in family, church, and local association—were deprived of life by an overweening federal state did the people, whether in city, town, or country, begin to abandon their duties. Even then, and even now, tens of millions of Americans seek to do their duties as husbands, wives, parents, parishioners, and citizens. But they now live alongside millions more who reject those duties as they reject the associations from which they spring.

America's history shows that issues of ethnicity and race need not preclude a functioning republic pursuing the people's common good. But habits generated over generations, some retaining local commitments, others casting them aside in favor of abstract goals like "social justice" and virtue-signaling orchestrated by elite-driven "narratives" cannot mesh together in one people. Perhaps the time has come to remember and reestablish the requirements for ordered liberty, including the requirement that the scope of government be relatively small and local—certainly smaller and more local than the leviathan that has grown between the seas and beyond and given birth to two very different patterns of thought, action, and moral reasoning.

Moreover, it is important to recognize that progressivism itself has reached its endgame. For the rationalistic formulae by which progressives justified the administrative state cannot stand up to the sheer resentment and will to power currently loose on the land. Identity politics has empowered antifa thugs, Black Lives Matters rioters, and critical race theory bullies. They have cowed progressives into public obeisance and administrative cooperation. This has meant adding yet another layer of bureaucracy, this one aimed at doling out life chances, status, and punishments according to victim status and adherence to current racial and sex-based vocabulary and "narratives." But this last layer of administration undermines the legitimacy of the entire edifice and burdens it in its financial and bureaucratic demands that the system cannot endure, indeed is crumbling all around us.

The last gasps of progressivism appear to be issuing from the barely conscious occupant of the White House. When Joe Biden manages to express himself coherently, he merely mimics the current, radical talking points. But he and his handlers keep the spigots open, printing ever-more money even as many Americans refuse to work and others can't find work because the costs of energy and materials have been so quickly and massively inflated amid lockdowns and ever-more-intrusive and unpredictable "woke" dictates.

This is how nations fall into chaos. The question is whether enough Americans will rediscover their unruly nature and so unmask their own true, historically rooted character in time to prevent the final loss of our way of life. Only clear action at school and county board meetings and throughout the public square as well as at the polls and the courts can allow Americans to take back their traditional powers of decentralized self-government under God.

Not long ago, some Americans were offended by a president who may have worked to protect our borders, our jobs, and our way of life but issued "mean tweets." Perhaps it is not too late to remember that our democratic culture and its politics are rooted as much in hard cider, tar, and feathers as in grand statements and appeasement masked as compromise. George Washington was not above providing food and strong drink to the people he wanted to vote for him. James Madison thought such acts beneath him; and so he failed to get elected—until he changed his mind and rolled out the cider barrels. Before we give up on America as one nation and perhaps seek to separate on amicable terms in a way that reflects our diverging characters, it seems worthwhile to set aside notions of civility that involve kid gloves and perpetual defeat. Perhaps it is time—peacefully to be sure—to rediscover the power of an unruly people.

NOTES

1. See for example the discussion of how elites perpetuate their class through their children's access to elite education and employment in Christopher Lasch, *Revolt of the Elites and the Betrayal of Democracy* (New York: Norton, 1995), ch. 3.

Conclusion

HONOR AMONG THE UNRULY

The irony of American character is this: a free republic requires instinctive adherence to the rule of law, but no law, no constitution, can protect a people's liberties if they are not willing and able to fight for them.

Our Constitution was designed to restrict the power of the majority and of powerful minorities. The overriding goal was to prevent tyranny, with its threats to the life, liberty, and property of its citizens while maintaining our character as a self-governing people. After many decades and many changes in our nation and people, the Constitution has proven insufficient to its task. The Framers' system of separated powers, maintained through checks and balances, has failed to provide a mechanism of restraint sufficient to prevent tyranny. Why not? Because something deeper than mechanisms is at play. To be free, a people must demand, protect, and above all exercise self-government. And this requires a certain character—vigorous, jealous, unruly, but also motivated by a combination of self-respect and a desire for the respect of others within one's community. That combination can be termed "honor" and it is essential to the character of a free people.

The very notion of American government as one of mixed, balanced, and separated powers can be taken as somewhat of a fiction because, in the end, all the power is vested in the People. No mechanism, no system of any kind, can prevent tyranny if the people itself does not hate tyranny and is not willing to prevent it. The fate of our constitutional republic rests with the people, which is to say American society as it responds to tyranny, including tyranny that gives Americans the comfort and aid they desire. The question yet to be answered, then, is whether Americans remain an honorable people. Republican honor emerged over time. It has roots in both an old English, aristocratic honor and nearly two centuries of local self-rule by a wide variety

181

of poor and middling Americans (with many ethnic variations) prior to the creation of the first large, national republic in history. What emerged over time is a peculiarly American character. This character was expressed in diverse regional and cultural varieties placing the self-respect born of self-reliance and self-rule at the center of both national and personal identity. It also gave to our constitutional system its life and its power to check tyranny. The mechanism was fitted to and made possible by the national character, it did not and could not forge that character, for laws that forge character are not the laws of a free people.

Politics in America, from its founding in Jamestown to 1607, was ruled by honor. Representatives of the people's will were mostly people who had cultivated a public character and reputation often associated with the "gentleman." Regional differences were profound and one can find many eruptions of the demagogue, but most communities operated with high levels of deference to those among them who had gained reputation for honor, public-spiritedness, and good character. The people of the community turned to such men to represent them because they believed they represented their own ideals, perhaps to a higher degree than others, and because men who had earned public respect were more capable than most of making wise, prudential judgments in the best interest of the community.

A representative, thus understood, is not expected to merely follow the dictates of popular whim. A representative of the people must be a leader, a guide, to the people. This widespread view of representation was not likely to survive unchanged after a bloody revolution fought in the name of popular sovereignty. The nature of the populations choosing their representatives changed rapidly, especially with the swift removal of loyalists from America. As important, the scale of power, and the stakes, became much larger. No one at the Constitutional Convention could have understood these forces or predicted how they would play out under the constitution they drafted. Rather, the political leaders of the new republic began with assumptions, beliefs, tactics, and customs already out of date.

Alexander Hamilton was among the first to pay for his mistaken judgment regarding the character of postindependence Americans. When an angry crowd gathered in New York City to protest the Jay Treaty, which secured peace and commerce with Great Britain at the cost of some American interests and pride, Hamilton circulated handbills appealing for calm and a serious examination of the Treaty. He expected, with some reason, that his reputation as a good and honorable man with a long history of devotion to the American cause would inspire the deference necessary for him to speak and explain his position. He did not hold that the people could not understand the issues or that they were incapable of being informed citizens. He simply assumed that they would listen to him because popular sovereignty implied a healthy deference to men of honor like him.

Hamilton was wrong. At the appointed time he mounted a stoop and began addressing the crowd, at which point he was silenced by rude noises. Continued efforts failed, eliciting only more hoots and a rock that hit Hamilton on the head. Hamilton left, unheard and disrespected. A gap had clearly developed between the norms of the recent past and emerging demands for a new kind of representation.

Hamilton's humiliation was no mere harbinger of "democratization"—of a demand by the citizens that their representatives be "like us." It was part of the development of the American character. That character includes a distinct lack of deference but it also entails a specific kind of republican honor.

Honor is a matter of esteem—in one's own eyes and in the eyes of those whom one respects. One must meet standards in one's own eyes even as one looks to figures who serve as examples of how those standards have been put into practice. An honorable person respects himself in several ways: he respects the standards for which he stands, he respects his ability to be self-reliant, and he respects his drive to meet his obligations to others—being a good neighbor and participating with others in self-rule.

If colonial Americans borrowed aristocratic forms of honor as they searched for fame and influence, the people of the new republic found in their own experiences and accomplishments the core ingredient to a new type of honor. They had long taken care of themselves, and they aimed to keep doing that. They respected their own accomplishments, took responsibility for their own failures, and developed the habits of mutual respect that would serve them well in the great community-building century of westward expansion that followed.

Like aristocratic honor, republican honor was far from universal, a great many people were dishonorable. But republican honor was, in fact, accessible to the many; it produced a nation of expansive freedom rooted in a system of self-regulation that kept a basic order among diverse people. We see clear but differing forms of honor in feuding families of the Appalachians and among those famous but misunderstood WASP patricians of nineteenth-century Philadelphia. But the varied systems of honor across American history had the virtue of self-respect that was earned through often difficult trials of depending on themselves, their families, and their communities rather than on experts, administrators, or some group of benevolent "betters" whose governance, whether well or ill administered, was demeaning to the governed.

The American concept of honor would develop over time, finding frontier expression in Davy Crockett or Andrew Jackson, but also in a more cultivated species in Abraham Lincoln and Frederick Douglass. Unlike the frontier version, in which one only had to look inside oneself to find the necessary virtues, Lincoln and Douglass, in what might be called the Whig or Republican species, stressed that self-education and self-cultivation were required of each person wishing to live well as a full person. Real self-rule, and the attending self-respect, were products of refinement and cultivation of our best selves, accomplished in many ways.

Self-improvement is an essential element, then, of American honor. Here we see the stuff of American myths—expressions of ourselves that we have long sought to live up to. Much, if not most, of American popular culture from the late nineteenth into the late twentieth century centered on code words like "individualism" and "self-made"; it evinced the power of the concept of the self-cultivated person who lives honorably because he respects himself and his ability to take care of himself with his neighbors and family.

The American, republican species of honor, then, expects government to provide the conditions that allow persons and families to be at liberty to pursue their lives based on their own choices and to do this largely within the context of their self-governing communities. The greatest internal danger to this honor is the development and spread of rule by administration. When Congress and other elected bodies are representatives of their constituents (and their constituents' interests) a self-respecting people can fight out differences in policy through elected governmental bodies. But when our government becomes our protector, when we defer to the judgment of administrators and other helping professionals to take care of us in realms we had long controlled ourselves, then the very conditions necessary for honor are destroyed. We become servants of a distant government that gives us what it deems in our best interests. Under such conditions we can no longer have the self-respect necessary for honor; we have given up any meaningful self-rule in favor of ease, safety, and comfort. We have relinquished the obligations that defined our character.

We see early signs of this development when we no longer feel the need to engage in self-cultivation relative to a higher ideal or version of ourselves, when we are no longer interested in an education that forms our best selves, instead favoring means (including education) that make us more rapacious consumers and more self-absorbed subjects of a rich nation. Once we have reached this stage, we no longer believe that taking care of ourselves is more noble than being cared for by a system that we do not control and cannot understand. We then give our children over to the state as if this discharges our obligation to educate our young because we expect the state to know better than we do what children should learn. We happily bequeath to the state the power to take care of the poor around us so long as we are protected from the consequences of our own bad choices. When distant and murky powers inside and outside government take responsibility for feeding us the information and versions of reality that violate our own experiences, we then know that we are subjects in a mere simulacrum of a self-governing republic.

This is where we find ourselves. The question, then, is whether we retain our honor. Do we have the self-respect to hold ourselves to higher standards, to assert our ability to be self-reliant, to demand that we be self-governing? If we accept our representatives' plans to take care of us we then cede our American right to take care of our own interests, to believe as we wish, to associate and to worship as we choose. If we comply with their plans, tolerating their assaults on our honor, then we no longer have reason to complain of our rulers. If we choose self-respect and demand our right of self-rule as both persons and groups, then the American Constitution, and the political culture it supports, will again be possible as lived realities.

The foundations of our Constitution, and our honor, concern how we carry out our responsibilities. Sending children to public schools that do not reflect our values. Ceding control over city councils, school boards, and local offices through inaction. Accepting the dictates of "experts" and the opinions of media and tech conglomerates as truth to be followed and enforced. These are the acts of a subject people.

Devoting ourselves to self-rule at the local level. Refusing to comply with administrative systems and rules that compel us to act, believe, assert, or merely comply against our standards and judgment. Resisting both the bland administrative apparatus and the vocal mobs and choosing self-respect and honor over a servile and comfortable life. These are the acts of a free, honorable, self-governing people.

In the end, a self-respecting, honorable, and self-governing people takes care of itself. Its members create the context in which they and those around them can cultivate the virtues and habits that lead to a good and honorable life. In some ways this entails beginning anew. But this is no time of mindless revolution. We begin anew by reconnecting with deep and abiding structures produced by hundreds of years of social and cultural development. We are called simply to be true to ourselves as Americans. Self-respect is the foundation of an honorable nation in which the citizens learn to be self-reliant and proudly self-governing.

Bibliography

A.L.A. Shecter Poultry Corp. v. U.S. 295 U.S. 495 (1935).

Allen, Michael. "No Christmas Display in Santa Monica, First Time in 60 Years." *Opposing Views,* last modified March 1, 2018, https://www.opposingviews.com/religion/churches-sue-christmas-displays-santa-monica-california.

Allen, Thomas B. *Tories: Fighting for the King in America's First Civil War* (New York: Harper, 2011), xx

Anderson, Sam. *Boomtown.* New York: Broadway, 2018.

Brenan, Megan. "Record-High 56% of U.S. Women Prefer Working to Homemaking." *Gallup,* October 24, 2019, https://news.gallup.com/poll/267737/record-high-women-prefer-working-homemaking.aspx.

Brown v. Board of Education 347 U.S. 483 (1954).

Calicchio, Dom. "Satanic display inside Illinois Statehouse days before Christmas draws protesters." *New York Post,* last modified December 23, 2021, https://nypost.com/2021/12/23/satanic-display-inside-illinois-statehouse-days-before-christmas-draws-protesters/ https://wsvn.com/news/local/satanic-display-included-in-boca-raton-holiday-parade/.

Conkin, Paul K. *Cane Ridge, America's Pentecost.* Madison: University of Wisconsin Press, 1990.

———. *A Requiem for the American Village.* Lanham: Rowman & Littlefield, 2000.

Dred Scott v. Sandford 60 U.S. (19 How.) 393 (1857).

Fischer, David Hackett. *Albion's Seed.* New York: Oxford University Press, 1996.

Frohnen, Bruce P., ed. *The American Republic.* Indianapolis: Liberty Fund, 2002.

Frohnen, Bruce P., and George W. Carey. *Constitutional Morality and the Rise of Quasi-Law.* Cambridge: Harvard University Press, 2016.

Haskell, Thomas L., and Richard F. Teichgraeber III, eds. *The Culture of the Market.* Cambridge: Cambridge University Press, 1996.

Healy, Patrick, and Daisy Lin. "Atheist Display Space Puts Squeeze on Santa Monica Nativity Scenes." NBC Los Angeles, last modified December 10, 2011, https://www.nbclosangeles.com/news/local/traditional-nativity-scenes-outnumbered-by-atheist-displays-in-santa-monica/1913885/.

Jeffrey, Terence. "Surge in welfare stems from rise in out-of-wedlock births." *Washington Examiner*, September 3, 2014, https://www.washingtonexaminer.com/surge-in-welfare-stems-from-rise-in-out-of-wedlock-births.

Jones, Jeffrey M. "U.S. Church Membership Down Sharply in Past Two Decades." Gallup, April 18, 2019, https://news.gallup.com/poll/248837/church-membership-down-sharply-past-two-decades.aspx.

Kirk, Russell. *The Roots of the American Order.* Wilmington: ISI Books, 2003.

Lasch, Christopher. *The Revolt of the Elites and the Betrayal of Democracy.* New York: Norton, 1995.

Lee v. Weisman, 505 U.S. 577 (1992).

Lewkowicz, Fabian. "Santa Monica Christmas Nativity Scene." *Santa Monica Closeup,* December 23, 2018, http://www.santamonicacloseup.com/home/2018/12/23/santa-monica-christmas-nativity-scene.html.

McAllister, Ted V., and Bruce P. Frohnen. *Coming Home: Reclaiming America's Conservative Soul.* New York: Encounter Books, 2019.

Murray, Charles. *Losing Ground.* New York: Basic, 2015.

Nisbet, Robert. *The Quest for Community.* Wilmington: ISI, 2010.

Novak, William. *The People's Welfare: Law and Regulation in Nineteenth-Century America.* Chapel Hill: University of North Carolina Press, 1996.

People v. Ruggles, 8 Johns. 290 (1811).

Plessy v. Ferguson 163 U.S. 537 (1896).

Putnam, Robert A. *Bowling Alone: The Collapse and Revival of American Community.* New York: Simon & Schuster, 2000.

Riesman, David, Nathan Glazer, and Reuel Denny. *The Lonely Crowd: A Study of the Changing American Character.* New York: Doubleday Anchor, 1953.

Romerstein, Herbert. *The Venona Secrets.* Washington, DC: Regnery, 2014.

Roosevelt, Franklin Delano. "Address Accepting the Presidential Nomination at the Democratic National Convention in Chicago." *The American Presidency Project,* July 2, 1932, https://www.presidency.ucsb.edu/documents/address-accepting-the-presidential-nomination-the-democratic-national-convention-chicago-1.

Schwartz, John E. *America's Hidden Success: A Reassessment of Public Policy from Kennedy to Reagan.* New York: Norton, 1987.

Students for a Democratic Society. *The Port Huron Statement.* http://www.progressivefox.com/misc_documents/PortHuronStatement.pdf.

Tocqueville, Alexis de. *Democracy in America.* Translated by Phillips Bradley. New York: Vintage, 1990.

Tyler, Alice Felt. *Freedom's Ferment: Phases of American Social History to 1860.* Tokyo: Case, 2007.

United States Census Bureau. "Colonial and Pre-Federal Statistics." 2004, https://www2.census.gov/prod2/statcomp/documents/CT1970p2-13.pdf.

Warren, Samuel, and Louis Brandeis. "The Right to Privacy," *Harvard Law Review* 4, no. 5 (December 15, 1890): 193–220.

Wesley, John. *Works,* vol. XIV. London: Wesleyan Conference, 1872.

Woodard, Colin. *American Nations: A History of the Eleven Rival Regional Cultures in North America.* New York: Penguin, 2012.

Further Reading

Alexander, Shawn Leigh. *Reconstruction Violence and the Ku Klux Klan Hearings.* Boston: Bedford/St. Martin's, 2015.

Aristotle. *Nicomachean Ethics.* Translated by Terence Irwin. Indianapolis: Hackett, 2019.

Berman, Harold J. *Law and Revolution: The Formation of the Western Legal Tradition.* Cambridge: Harvard University Press, 1985.

———. *Law and Revolution II: The Impact of the Protestant Reformations on the Western Legal Tradition.* Cambridge: Harvard University Press, 2006.

Blight, David W. *Frederick Douglass: Prophet of Freedom.* New York: Simon & Schuster, 2020.

Boorstin, Daniel J. *The Americans: The Colonial Experience.* New York: Vintage, 1964.

———. *The Americans: The Democratic Experience.* New York: Vintage, 1974.

———. *The Americans: The National Experience.* New York: Vintage Books, 1967.

Burnham, Daniel. *The Managerial Revolution.* New York: John Day, 1941.

Caldwell, Christopher. *The Age of Entitlement: America Since the Sixties.* New York: Simon & Schuster, 2020.

Carey, George W., and James McClellan, eds. *The Federalist.* Indianapolis: Liberty Fund, 2001.

Carlson, Allan C. *"The American Way."* Wilmington: ISI, 2003.

———. *From Cottage to Work Station.* San Francisco: Ignatius, 1993.

Caro, Robert A. *Lyndon Johnson: The Passage of Power.* New York: Knopf, 2012.

Commager, Henry Steele, ed. *Living Ideas in America.* New York: Harper, 1951.

Crockett, David. *Davy Crockett: His Own Story.* Corona: Applewood, 1993.

Ehrenhalt, Alan. *The Lost City: The Forgotten Virtues of Community in America.* New York: Basic, 1995.

Fitzgerald, Michael W. *Splendid Failure: Postwar Reconstruction in the American South.* Chicago: Ivan R. Dee, 2008.

Foner, Eric. *Reconstruction.* New York: Harper, 2014.

Ford, Lacy K. *Deliver us from Evil: The Slavery Question in the Old South.* Oxford: Oxford University Press, 2009.

Freehling, William W. *The Road to Disunion, v. II: Secessionists Triumphant.* Oxford: Oxford University Press, 2007.

Freeman, Joanne B. *Affairs of Honor: National Politics in the New Republic.* New Haven: Yale University Press, 2002.

———. *The Field of Blood: Violence in Congress and the Road to Civil War.* New York: Picador, 2019.

Frohnen, Bruce P., ed. *The American Nation.* Indianapolis: Liberty Fund, 2009.

Fulsom, Burton W. *The Myth of the Robber Barons.* Santa Barbara: Young America's Foundation, 2018.

Goodwyn, Lawrence. *Democratic Promise: The Populist Moment in America.* Oxford: Oxford University Press, 1976.

Hamburger, Philip. *Law and Judicial Duty.* Cambridge: Harvard University Press, 2009.

———. *Separation of Church and State.* Cambridge: Harvard University Press, 2004.

Hobbes, Thomas. *Leviathan.* Indianapolis: Hackett, 1994.

Hofstadter, Richard. *The Age of Reform.* New York: Vintage, 1955.

Hofstadter, Richard, ed., *The Progressive Movement.* Englewood Cliffs: Prentice-Hall, 1963.

Holton, Woody. *Unruly Americans and the Origins of the Constitution.* New York: Hill & Wang, 2008.

Horwitz, Morton J. *The Transformation of American Law.* Cambridge: Harvard University Press, 1979.

Howe, Daniel Walker. *Making the American Self: Jonathan Edwards to Abraham Lincoln.* Cambridge: Harvard University Press, 1997.

———. *What Hath God Wrought? The Transformation of America, 1810–1848.* Oxford: Oxford University Press, 2009.

Josephson, Matthew. *The Robber Barons.* New York: Harper, 1962.

Kendall, Willmoore, and George W. Carey. *The Basic Symbols of the American Political Tradition.* Washington: Catholic University of America Press, 1995.

Kirk, Russell. *Rights and Duties: Reflections on Our Conservative Constitution.* Dallas: Spence, 1997.

Litwack, Leon F. *Trouble in Mind: Black Southerners in the Age of Jim Crow.* New York: Knopf, 1998.

Locke, John. *Two Treatises of Civil Government.* Cambridge: Cambridge University Press, 1988.

Lutz, Donald S. *The Origins of American Constitutionalism.* Baton Rouge: Louisiana State University Press, 1988.

May, Henry F. *The Enlightenment in America.* Oxford: Oxford University Press, 1978.

McClain, Edward B. *The Most Dangerous Branch.* Lanham: University Press of America, 2008.

McClay, Wilfred M. *Land of Hope: An Invitation to the Great American Story.* New York: Encounter, 2020.

———. *The Masterless: Self and Society in Modern America.* Chapel Hill: University of North Carolina Press, 1994.

Onuf, Peter S. *Statehood and Union: A History of the Northwest Ordinance.* Notre Dame: University of Notre Dame Press, 2019.

Pestritto, Ronald J. *America Transformed: The Rise and Legacy of American Progressivism.* New York: Encounter, 2021.

Prince, K. Stephen. *Radical Reconstruction.* Boston: Bedford/St. Martin's, 2016.

Rosenberg, Gerald N. *The Hollow Hope: Can Courts Bring About Social Change?* Chicago: University of Chicago Press, 2008.

Rossiter, Clinton. *Conservatism in America: The Thankless Persuasion.* New York: Vintage, 1961.

Shlaes, Amity. *The Forgotten Man: A New History of the Great Depression.* New York: Harper, 2008.

Smith, Helena Huntington. *The War on Powder River.* Lincoln: University of Nebraska Press, 1967.

Starr, Kevin. *Americans and the California Dream.* Oxford: Oxford University Press, 1986.

Thaler, Richard H. and Cass R. Sunstein. *Nudge: Improving Decisions About Health, Wealth, and Happiness.* New Haven: Yale University Press, 2008.

Thompson, Bob. *Born on a Mountaintop: On the Road with Davy Crockett and the Ghosts of the Wild Frontier.* New York: Crown, 2014.

Wallis, Michael. *David Crockett: The Lion of the West.* New York: Norton, 2012.

Watson, Bradley C. S. *Diversity, Conformity, and Conscience in Contemporary America.* Lanham: Lexington Books, 2021.

Weber, Max. *The Protestant Ethic and the Spirit of Capitalism and Other Writings.* Translated by Peter Baehr and Gordon C. Wells. New York: Penguin, 2002.

Wilder, Laura Ingalls. *The Long Winter.* New York: Harper Collins, 2008.

Wills, Shomari. *Black Fortunes: The Story of the First Six African Americans Who Escaped Slavery and Became Millionaires.* New York: Amistad, 2019.

Wolf, Eva Sheppard. *Race and Liberty in the New Nation.* Baton Rouge: Louisiana State University Press, 2009.

Index

About the Authors

Bruce P. Frohnen is professor of law at the Ohio Northern University College of Law and Senior Fellow at the Russell Kirk Center for Cultural Renewal. He coauthored *Coming Home: Reclaiming America's Conservative Soul* (Encounter, 2019) with Ted V. McAllister and *Constitutional Morality and the Rise of Quasi-Law* (Harvard, 2016) with George W. Carey and is the author of *Virtue and the Promise of Conservatism: The Legacy of Burke and Tocqueville* (Kansas, 1993) and *The New Communitarians and the Crisis of Modern Liberalism* (Kansas, 1996). Among his edited works is a two-volume set of primary sources, *The American Republic* (Liberty Fund, 2002) and *The American Nation* (Liberty Fund, 2009) used widely in various schools and universities and frequently cited in academic journals and judicial opinions. He has published several hundred articles, essays, and reviews in publications including the *Harvard Journal of Law & Public Policy* and the *American Journal of Jurisprudence.*

Ted V. McAllister is the Edward L. Gaylord Chair and professor of public policy at Pepperdine School of Public Policy. In addition to serving as principal coauthor of *Coming Home,* he is the author of *Revolt Against Modernity: Leo Strauss, Eric Voegelin, and the Search for a Post-Liberal Order* (Kansas, 1996, Portuguese Brazilian edition, E REALIZACOES 2017) and editor, with Wilfred McClay, of *Why Place Matters: Geography, Identity, and Civic Life in Modern America* (New Atlantis, 2014). His work appears in a variety of academic and popular journals, and he lectures widely on themes ranging from Alexis de Tocqueville to Eric Voegelin to the debate about the nature of American identity.